# 2nd Workshop on Computing News Storylines (CNS 2016)

Held at the Conference on Empirical Methods in Natural Language Processing (EMNLP 2016)

Austin, Texas, USA
5 November 2016

ISBN: 978-1-5108-3149-0

# Introduction

This volume contains the proceedings of the 2nd Workshop on Computing News Storylines (CNewsStory 2016) held in conjunction with the 2016 Conference on Empirical Methods in Natural Language Processing (EMNLP 2016) in Austin, Texas, USA, on 5 November 2016. Narratives are at the heart of information sharing. Ever since people began to share their experiences, they have connected them to form narratives. The study of storytelling and the field of literary theory called narratology have developed complex frameworks and models related to various aspects of narrative such as plots structures, narrative embeddings, characters' perspectives, reader response, point of view, narrative voice, narrative goals, and many others. These notions from narratology have been applied mainly in Artificial Intelligence and to model formal semantic approaches to narratives (e.g. Plot Units developed by Lehnert (1981)). In recent years, computational narratology has qualified as an autonomous field of study and research. Narrative has been the focus of a number of workshops and conferences (AAAI Symposia, Interactive Storytelling Conference (ICIDS), Computational Models of Narrative). Furthermore, reference annotation schemes for narratives have been proposed (NarrativeML by Mani (2013)).

The workshop aims to bring together researchers from different communities working on representing and extracting narrative structures in news, a text genre popular in NLP research but which has received little attention in research into narrative structure, representation and analysis.

Current advances in NLP technology have made it possible to look beyond scenario-driven, atomic extraction of events from single documents and work towards extracting story structures from multiple documents, while these documents are published over time as news streams. Policy makers and information specialists are increasingly in need of tools that support them in finding salient stories in large amounts of information to more effectively implement policies, monitor actions of "big players" in society and check facts. Their tasks often revolve around reconstructing cases either with respect to specific entities (e.g. person or organisations) or events (e.g. the 2016 presidential elections). Storylines represent explanatory schemas that enable us to make better selections of relevant information but also projections for the future. They constitute a huge potential for exploiting news data in an innovative way.

Of the 14 submissions we received, 8 were accepted that touch upon different aspects of narrative research in news. Three contributions describe approaches to detect storylines either from news (Brüggermann et al.), from Tweets (Krishnan and Eisenstein), or from news but with metadata added via Twitter (Poghosyan and Ifrim). Besides detecting storylines, different aspects of storylines such as diegesis and point of view are also addressed (Eisenberg and Finlayson). The second topic that is addressed is annotation and representation of storylines (Caselli and Vossen and O'Gorman et al.). Related to this is the analysis of the distribution of narrative schemas in a corpus, which may help further the discussion on corpus creation (Simonson and Davis). Finally, ideas on how to put storylines to use in a newsroom are discussed in Caswell.

We would like to thank the members of the Program Committee for their timely reviews and the authors for their contributions.

**Organizers:**

Tommaso Caselli, Vrije Universiteit Amsterdam
Ben Miller, Georgia State University
Marieke van Erp, Vrije Universiteit Amsterdam
Piek Vossen, Vrije Universiteit Amsterdam
David Caswell, Reynolds Journalism Institute & University of Missouri

**Program Committee:**

Alexandra Balahur, European Commission Joint Research Centre, Ispra, Italy
Sabine Bergler, Computer Science, Columbia University, Canada
Matje van de Camp, De Taalmonsters, The Netherlands
Reginald Chua, Thomson Reuters, USA
Leon Derczynski, University of Sheffield, UK
Mark Finlayson, Florida International University, USA
Martijn Kleppe, Koninklijke Bibliotheek, Den Haag, The Netherlands
Bernardo Magnini, HLT-FBK, Italy
Roser Morante, Vrije Universiteit Amsterdam, The Netherlands
Nasrin Mostafazadeh, University of Rochester, USA
Vivi Nastase, Institut fur Computerlinguistik, University of Heidelberg, Germany
Silvia Pareti, Google Inc. & University of Edinburgh
Octavian Popescu, IBM Watson Research Center, USA
Ellen Riloff, University of Utah, USA
Jonathan Stray, Columbia University, USA
Xavier Tannier, LIMSI-CNRS, France
Marc Verhagen, Brandeis University, USA

**Invited Speaker:**

Eduard Hovy - Bridging the Gap between Event Macro-structures and Event Micro-structures
Carnegie Mellon University

# Table of Contents

vii

# Workshop Program

**Saturday, November 5, 2016**

**09:00–10:30**  **Session 1: Opening Session**

**09:00–09:10**  *Welcome and Opening Remarks*

09:10–10:10  *Bridging the Gap between Event Macro-structures and Event Micro-structures*
Ed Hovy, Language Technologies Institute, CMU

**10:30–11:00**  *Coffee Break*

**11:00–12:30**  **Session 2: Morning Session**

11:00–11:25  *Computable News Ecosystems: Roles for Humans and Machines*
David Caswell

11:25–11:50  *Storyline detection and tracking using Dynamic Latent Dirichlet Allocation*
Daniel Bruggermann, Yannik Hermey, Carsten Orth, Darius Schneider, Stefan
Selzer and Gerasimos Spanakis

11:50–12:15  *Real-time News Story Detection and Tracking with Hashtags*
Gevorg Poghosyan and Georgiana Ifrim

12:15–12:30  *Nonparametric Bayesian Storyline Detection from Microtexts*
Vinodh Krishnan and Jacob Eisenstein

**12:30–14:00**  *Lunch*

**Saturday, November 5, 2016 (continued)**

**14:00–15:30    Session 3: Afternoon Session**

14:00–14:25    *Automatic Identification of Narrative Diegesis and Point of View*
Joshua Eisenberg and Mark Finlayson

14:25–14;50    *Richer Event Description: Integrating event coreference with temporal, causal and bridging annotation*
Tim O'Gorman, Kristin Wright-Bettner and Martha Palmer

14:50–15:15    *NASTEA: Investigating Narrative Schemas through Annotated Entities*
Dan Simonson and Anthony Davis

15:15–15:30    *The Storyline Annotation and Representation Scheme (StaR): A Proposal*
Tommaso Caselli and Piek Vossen

**16:00–17:00    Session 4: Discussion and Closing Remarks**

# Computable News Ecosystems: Roles for Humans and Machines

**David Caswell**

Reynolds Journalism Institute, Missouri School of Journalism, Columbia, MO

## Abstract

Two contrasting paradigms for structuring news events and storylines are identified and described: the automated paradigm and the manual paradigm. A specific manual news structuring system is described, and the high-level results of three reporting experiments conducted using the system are presented. In light of these results I then compare automated and manual approaches and argue that they are complementary. A proposal for integrating automated and manual techniques within a structured news ecosystem is presented, and recommendations for integrated approaches are provided.

## 1 Introduction

News is produced and consumed within local, national and global ecosystems. These ecosystems are made up of large numbers of diverse organizations and individuals, playing a variety of roles: newspapers, news websites, television channels, wire services, aggregators, specialty publishers, sources, freelance reporters, bloggers, social media contributors, advertisers, business and government intelligence organizations, individual news consumers and many others. These ecosystem participants collectively create, remix, exchange, distribute and consume vast quantities of information, almost entirely as discrete blocks of natural language in the form of text articles or scripted video segments.

News ecosystems are currently being disrupted by the internet-driven democratization of publishing and the resulting commodification of text and video (Anderson et al., 2014). This commodification has damaged the economic foundations of news producers, but it has also dramatically increased the depth and breadth of news available to consumers. Unfortunately it is difficult for news consumers to take full advantage of this increased quantity of news, because of the difficulty of converting the information content of large numbers of text articles or video segments into coherent narratives necessary for human understanding (Holton and Chyi, 2012). Overwhelming quantities of text articles and the resulting sense-making challenge for news consumers have been partially addressed by search, personalized article ranking, collaborative filtering, social media curation and other approaches, however, while useful, these technologies have not solved the text overload problem.

A new approach to this sense-making challenge is emerging. It proposes replacing the text article as the primary 'unit of news' with new information artifacts that are aligned with human models of narrative coherence but which are also directly computable. These information artifacts are typically forms of structured 'storylines', in which news events and narratives are recorded as structured representations based on ontologies of semantic frames or event abstractions, each containing well-defined semantic roles. Actual news events can then be instantiated by 'filling in' these semantic roles with references to nodes within knowledge graphs. These structured records of events are then organized into storyline structures that exhibit characteristics of coherent narratives, such as semantic zoom, differential value of events and networked interconnection.



*Proceedings of 2nd Workshop on Computing News Storylines*, pages 1–8,
Austin, TX, November 5, 2016. ©2016 Association for Computational Linguistics

By structuring news and making it directly available for computation it becomes possible to develop novel news products that are more efficient vehicles for human understanding than corpora of text articles, including summarizations, interactive interfaces, personalized news delivery, query tools, question answering, analytics, etc.

The most common paradigm proposed for this new approach is one of automation, specifically of automated reading (Strassel et al., 2010). This paradigm holds that the source of news events and narratives is in vast corpora and continuous streams of text articles, and that the creation of structured news storylines requires systematically examining those text articles with various natural language processing tools in order to automatically identify and de-duplicate news events across documents, and organize those events into structured storylines based on common locations, characters and entities. The automation paradigm is well-aligned with the current preference within software development for statistical and machine learning approaches to knowledge engineering tasks. This paradigm is also aligned with many previous research projects on computational narratives (Mani, 2013)(Chambers and Jurafsky, 2008)(Zarri, 2009), which often assumed text as the source of narratives and sought the representation of those text narratives as their objective.

This position paper proposes a different paradigm. I describe the operation and evaluation of a manual structured news platform, called 'Structured Stories', and I draw on that experience to examine the potential for human editorial workflows in directly structuring news. I argue that human editorial judgement is essential for creating and maintaining high-quality structured storylines and can be feasibly applied at ecosystem scales. The paper also reviews both paradigms from an ecosystem perspective, and identifies complementary opportunities for both approaches within a computable news ecosystem.

## 2   Automated Structuring of News

The automated construction of structured storylines from corpora of text articles is challenging because of the absence of any theory of natural language that might formalize the recovery of meaning across documents, or even across sentence boundaries within a single document (Hauser et al., 2002). Without such a theory the event and narrative information contained within natural language text must be extracted indirectly, using an array of Natural Language Processing (NLP) tools. This extraction typically requires identifying discrete news events from references to action within text, capturing those events and their participants as semantic frames and associated semantic roles, de-duplicating the events from other references found in other texts, and then organizing the structured events in context within structured storylines using time, location, common entities or cause-and-effect relationships. None of these steps is trivial and errors compound across all steps, but NLP tools such as frame parsers and named entity recognition (NER) have substantially improved the state of the art.

Automated news reading systems have been attempted in university environments since the 1970s (Cullingford, 1978), however practical, scalable products capable of constructing structured storylines from corpora or streams of news articles have only recently been achieved. Two of these systems, GDELT and EventRegistry (Kwak and An, 2016), are essentially databases of news events structured using relatively coarse ontologies of event abstractions and semantic roles, and supporting only simplified storylines based on time, location or common entities. A third system, called NewsReader, supports more complex storylines, including causal chains, and also includes information about pre- and post-event 'states' within its ontology (Rospocher et al., 2016).

These pioneering systems have successfully demonstrated that it is possible to automatically read large corpora or streams of text news articles, individuate discrete news events, and organize them into explorable structured storylines. These structured storylines are clearly useful and can be deployed at scale, but they convey only a tiny fraction of the information available from storylines conveyed using natural language, and they are also subject to a range of errors. The resolution and quality of these structured events and storylines will improve as the NLP technologies upon which they depend improves, however there may be limits to resolution and quality achievable from statistical NLP techniques (Hovy, 2016), and those limits may be substantially below levels necessary for these structured storylines to replace natural language text as units of news within news ecosystems.

## 3 Manual Structuring of News

'Structured writing' is an alternative to the automated reading paradigm for generating structured news storylines. The structured writing paradigm holds that the source of news events and narratives is in human editorial judgement - existing understanding that resides in the minds of skilled and informed journalists or analysts. Like automated reading systems, structured writing systems provide an ontology of event abstractions with which to structure news events and assemble storylines, but they require human operators, using dedicated interfaces and tools, to decide which news events to encode as structure, which entities fill the semantic roles within those events, and how those events are organized into storylines. Although they have similar utility, and are based on similar structured representations, structured writing systems differ from automated reading systems in that they exhibit advantages and disadvantages associated with human-centered workflows.

The Structured Stories platform (Caswell, 2015) is an example of a structured writing system. This platform was designed primarily as a knowledge representation system for general news, at a level of semantic granularity substantially finer than representation schemes designed for automated systems, such as NewsReader's Events and Situations Ontology, or GDELT's ontology. The semantic foundation used in the Structured Stories ontology is FrameNet (Baker, 2008), and the additional semantic resolution is added by enabling controlled extension of the FrameNet ontology to form journalistic 'event frames'. Actual news events are then instantiated by assigning knowledge graph references to the semantic roles within these event frames. The platform provides an organization scheme for arranging structured events into structured narratives, including a recursive 'sub-narrative' mechanism to provide semantic zoom and a differential value mechanism for detail management. The resulting structured narratives are assembled from references to events, forming a multi-dimensional graph from common events, common characters, common entities, common locations, etc. Event entry by human reporters is achieved using a simplified sequential user interface that is initiated by the selection of a verb and completed by sequential menu selections that enable the reporter to assign references to the semantic roles, provide time/duration, location, etc. The consumption of structured storylines from the Structured Stories database is enabled by a range of interactive techniques, including timelines, flowcharts, image slideshows, bullet points and text articles generated using natural language generation technology. These interactive techniques are delivered via different user interfaces, including a database management interface, an image-centered interface and a mobile interface.

The feasibility of using human reporters to report directly into the Structured Stories platform was assessed during 2015 and early 2016 in three major reporting projects employing a total of 10 reporters. All of these projects reported real-world news, and reporters were not substantially restricted in what they could choose to report. One was conducted as a stand-alone project with full-time reporters under the guidance of a senior editor (Caswell et al., 2015), one was conducted at a major school of journalism, and one was conducted in the newsroom of a major media company. In aggregate this assessment generated about 120 individual structured storylines, containing about 2300 structured events encoded using about 530 event frames and involving about 1100 different participants (characters, entities, locations, etc.). The level of semantic granularity of the structured events was loosely equivalent to that of the primary events reported in informational articles in a regional newspaper (typically 2-3 events per article), and therefore the assessment produced the event information equivalent of approximately 920 de-duplicated text articles. By comparison the Wall Street Journal produces about 240 articles per day (Meyer, 2016), many of which substantially duplicate events across articles.

This experience of manually reporting structured events into the Structured Stories platform produced several high-level results. The granularity of the event representation scheme was sufficient to capture almost all news events that the reporters wanted to report, suggesting that FrameNet is now relatively comprehensive and that the extension to event frames is relatively practical. All reporters were able to individuate discrete news events, to structure those events appropriately and to assemble storylines from those structured events, however there was wide variability in the ability of reporters to do so. Of the ten reporters three adapted very quickly to the process and became very productive within days, four adapted more slowly, requiring experience and feedback to gradually achieve a moderate level of productivity, and three were unable to adapt and remained at a relatively low level of productivity. Based on post-project interviews it appears that the determining factor in a reporter's ability to adapt to the structuring of news may be their general comfort with abstraction. The actual structuring of events by reporters using the user interface appeared to be relatively easy, typically requiring only 1-2 minutes per event, however the reporting and decision making about events and their semantic roles and characteristics was much more time-consuming. Some reporters described experiencing significant boredom in approaching journalism in this way, and some described a loss of satisfaction in being 'arrangers' of news rather than originators of news using traditional journalistic practices. Nonetheless most reporters saw promise in the technique and thought that it might appeal to some journalists, especially with improvements to the user interface and to the editorial workflow.

Other examples of manual systems for structuring news exist. A major research effort has been ongoing at the BBC since 2010, centered on their News Storyline Ontology (Rissen et al., 2013). This ontology is simpler than the Structured Stories ontology and is intended to be eventually used by reporters as part of regular journalism operations at the BBC, and as part of broader recording of the global news activity by the BBC Monitoring team. Another example is Circa (Coddington, 2015), a San Francisco-based news start-up that was founded in 2010 and closed in 2015 and which used a 10-person editorial team to manually structure journalism into discrete 'atomic units' of news, including events, and assemble those 'atoms' into structured storylines. Other, similar, attempts at manually structuring events exist outside of journalism, including the Nano-publication movement (Mons and Velterop, 2009), which seeks to complement or replace scientific publishing using text papers with much more granular 'nano publications' expressed as RDF triples, from which large-scale networked knowledge structures can be assembled. Nano-publication assumes 'crowdsourced' structuring of research results, in which researchers manually structure their own results. Each of these projects is exploring the feasibility of manually creating and curating repositories of semantically-structured storyline-like information artifacts that originate directly as structure rather than as features extracted from text.

The efficiency of data entry into the Structured Stories platform and into other manual news-structuring systems could be substantially improved in several ways. There is a large and growing body of news that is already available as structured data and which could be mapped into structured events and storylines, including sports news, financial news and increasingly large portions of political news. There are novel techniques based on Controlled Natural Language (Schwitter, 2010) that may enable structured events and storylines to be entered using forms of written language that are more familiar to journalists and analysts. There are also clearly opportunities for at least partial automation of event identification and individuation, using tools and techniques developed for fully-automated news structuring.

## 4  Comparison

The automatic and manual paradigms for structuring news are complementary. The underlying knowledge representation schemes with which they record structured news events and storylines are broadly similar, and the approaches can therefore be considered as different input mechanisms to a single structured news database. The advantages of each method generally address the disadvantages of the other, suggesting that integrating manual and automated approaches is desirable. Similar approaches, which combine machine learning with human decision-making and oversight, are sometimes called 'human-in-the-loop' (HITL) systems and are increasingly being applied in commercial environments (Bridgwater, 2016).

The primary advantage of manual news structuring is that it enables the application of human editorial judgement in event entry and in the creation and editing of storylines. This has numerous benefits, including the ability to substantially increase the semantic granularity of the represented news events, the ability to avoid and correct errors, the ability to anticipate the needs of consumers, the ability to easily handle unusual events or storyline situations, the ability to handle ambiguity, easily de-duplicate events, etc. The primary disadvantage of manual news structuring is the limited scale at which structuring can be done - i.e. the number and breadth of events and storylines that can be structured - and the lack of consistency with which structuring can be done. Other disadvantages arise from the cultural and workflow challenges inherent in using relatively high-skill human reporters or analysts to perform relatively unsatisfying tasks, as observed in the Structured Stories reporting experiments.

The primary advantage of automated news structuring is the scale of news structuring that can be achieved and the consistency by which that structuring can be done. It is possible, for example, to continually scan the entire global news stream, about 5 million text news articles per day (Wedenberg and Sjberg, 2014), and to detect, de-duplicate and structure major news events for insertion into storylines. The challenges of building and deploying automated news structuring tools are significant, however. There are a series of technical challenges in key tasks, including event detection, assignment of semantic roles, de-duplication of events and organization of structured events into storylines. Each of these can be done, but only with relatively high error rates and at relatively simplistic semantic granularity of the structured events. Storylines produced by automated systems are relatively simplistic and may not be engaging enough for broad communication of news to consumers beyond decision-makers with strong information needs. Furthermore, as the economic basis of professional news organizations erodes, automated news structuring approaches are facing a rapid deterioration in the quality of the corpus of text news articles from which they source news events. This reduction in corpus quality is occurring simultaneously with an increase in the quantity of digital text artifacts, thereby forcing automated systems to detect less semantic signal embedded in more semantic noise.

A comparison of automated and manual approaches to structuring news also reveals differing assumptions about the nature of storylines, and of stories generally. The automated approach loosely assumes that storylines are objective features that already exist in reality (or at least in the source corpus) and that must be found or discovered. The manual approach loosely assumes that storylines are necessarily human-created artifacts, with a human purpose, and that therefore there cannot be a story without an author or authors. This is an important distinction, because it determines whether computational storylines are mechanisms that are primarily useful for search in text corpora or mechanisms that are primarily useful for the storage and communication of human understanding. An automated approach to structuring news is essentially a kind of search engine, albeit one that can deliver unusual and valuable results and therefore aid humans in building understanding. In contrast a news structuring method that is subject to human editing, judgement and oversight could directly accumulate the understanding of skilled and informed journalists and analysts and could refine that understanding over time.

## 5 Computable News as an ecosystem

It is useful to consider the end-to-end creation, management and use of structured news storylines as an ecosystem, or at least as a highly modular system, because such a view encourages the application of automated or manual techniques as appropriate to the common objective of managing news as structured semantic data rather than as collections of text articles. The possible ecosystem described below (and shown in Figure 1) is hypothetical only regarding the integration of its various components, each of which have already been developed, deployed and evaluated in various stand-alone experimental and commercial systems.

A structured news ecosystem would be centered on a single schema for representing news events and storylines as structure, deployed either as multiple interconnected news databases or possibly as a single centralized news database. A wide variety of sources and methods for capturing news events as structure and for entering them into structured storylines within those databases would be deployed, including manual, semi-automated and entirely automated methods. Manual methods could include sequential user interfaces, such as that used in Structured Stories, controlled natural language interfaces, managed crowdsourcing similar to Wikipedia's editorial process and the use of task marketplaces such as Amazon's Mechanical Turk. Semi-automated methods could include workflows that automatically parse events and semantic roles from text, and presented them to human reporter/analysts for verification. Fully automated methods would include the automated parsing of simple, easily-identified events from text in web corpora, the detection of events in raw structured data and the mapping of events from existing structured event data. These various input methods would be only loosely coupled to the data repository, and new sources of structured news events would be integrated as they were developed.

Regardless of the sources of structured news data, it would be necessary for the resulting structured news database(s) to be under human editorial supervision. This is essential for detecting and responding to errors, for handling unusual events or situations, for enabling the use of events of finer semantic granularity than could be handled automatically, for applying judgement about sub-narratives and detail management, for assessing and managing the various event input methods, and for ensuring the coherence of storylines. The burden of such supervision could be managed using various automated processes and analytical tools while retaining human editorial authority over the overall structured dataset.

The methods of using and consuming structured news events and storylines from a news database would also be varied and modular. Simple interactive interfaces, such as lists, timelines, flowcharts, slideshows, cards, etc. would be necessary, as would basic query and search tools. The available semantic structure would also enable advanced interactive interfaces, especially 'chat bot' interfaces that deliver detailed question-answering. Other advanced interfaces could also be integrated, such as on-demand text articles produced using Natural Language Gen-

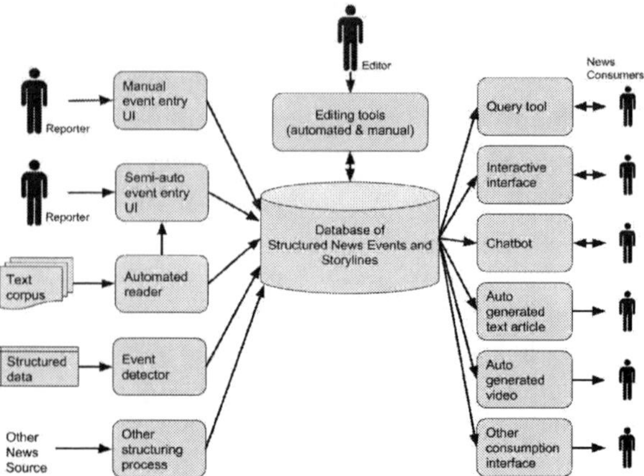



**Figure 1:** An integrated structured news ecosystem.

erations (NLG) tools (Graefe, 2016), automatically generated comics, or on-demand video segments produced using automated video production tools (Kay, 2015).

All of these components already exist and have been deployed in experimental and commercial systems, therefore the technical challenges of assembling an integrated manual/automated structured news ecosystem would primarily involve integration. The human factor and cultural challenges would probably be more difficult, however there is substantial motivation within existing news organizations to find new ways of automating, bundling and exploiting news. These organizations already have a trained workforce of many tens of thousands of skilled reporters and editors, and it appears from the Structured Stories reporting experiments that portions of this workforce may have the analytical and abstraction skills necessary to transition to new 'meta-journalism' or 'meta-editorial' roles within a structured news environment.

## 6 Conclusions

The existing text-based news ecosystem is failing for both producers and consumers of news, and novel structured and automated approaches to news are required. The assumption that news events and storylines originate in natural language text and that automated reading is the sole method available to access and structure those events and storylines is limiting. Lessons from the Structured Stories reporting experiments, and from other manual news structuring projects, have shown that applying human editorial judgement to structured news environments is feasible, and can potentially address some of the weaknesses of fully automated systems. Integration of automated and manual approaches to structuring news could enable a structured news ecosystem that exhibits the advantages of each method.

Facilitating the development of a structured news ecosystem requires viewing computable news functionality as modular, with manual, semi-automated and automated components. Integration of these modular components within an ecosystem will require standards - particularly a standard representation schema for structured news events and storylines, and standard interfaces for event entry modules and for storyline consumption modules. Addressing the human factors challenges of an integrated structured news ecosystem will require development of the abstraction skills of reporters, editors and analysts and enabling journalists to practice their profession at a higher level of abstraction. These are not simple challenges, however the experience of building and evaluating both automated and manual news structuring systems has demonstrated that they are achievable.

## Acknowledgments

The author would like to acknowledge support for the Structured Stories project from the Reynolds Journalism Institute at the Missouri School of Journalism, The Reporter's Lab at Duke University and the Online News Association Challenge Fund.

## References

C.W. Anderson, Emily Bell, and Clay Shirky. 2014. Post industrial journalism: Adapting to the present. Technical report, Tow Center for Digital Journalism, New York, NY.

Collin Baker. 2008. Framenet, present and future. *Proceedings of the First International Conference on Global Interoperability for Language Resources.*

Adrian Bridgwater. 2016. Machine learning needs a human-in-the-loop. *Forbes*, March.

David Caswell, Frank Russell, and Bill Adair. 2015. Editorial aspects of reporting into structured narratives. *Proceedings of the 2015 Computation + Journalism Symposium.*

David Caswell. 2015. Structured narratives as a framework for journalism: A work in progress. *Proceedings of the Sixth International Workshop on Computational Models of Narrative.*

Nathanael Chambers and Dan Jurafsky. 2008. Unsupervised learning of narrative event chains. In *Proceedings of ACL-08: HLT*, pages 789–797. Association for Computational Linguistics.

Mark Coddington. 2015. *Telling Secondhand Stories: News Aggregation and the Production of Journalistic Knowledge*. Ph.D. thesis, The University of Texas at Austin, Austin, TX.

Richard Edward Cullingford. 1978. Script application: Computer understanding of newspaper stories. Technical report, Yale University, New Haven, CT.

Andreas Graefe. 2016. Guide to automated journalism. Technical report, Tow Center for Digital Journalism, New York, NY.

Marc Hauser, Noam Chomsky, and Tecumseh Fitch. 2002. The faculty of language: What is it, who has it, and how did it evolve? *Science*, 298:1569–1579.

Avery E. Holton and Hsiang Iris Chyi. 2012. News and the overloaded consumer: Factors influencing information overload among news consumers. *Cyberpsychology, Behavior, and Social Networking*, 15:619–624, November.

Eduard Hovy. 2016. Filling the long tail. Keynote presentation of the 2nd Spinoza Workshop: Looking at the Long Tail, Vrije Universiteit Amsterdam, June.

Hilary Kay. 2015. This is how text-to-video technology works. Technical report, Wibbitz Inc.

Haewoon Kwak and Jisun An. 2016. Comparison of widely used world news datasets: Gdelt and eventregistry. *Proceedings of the 23rd International Conference on Web and Social Media.*

Inderjeet Mani. 2013. *Computational Modeling of Narrative*. Morgan and Claypool, San Rafael, CA.

Robinson Meyer. 2016. How many stories do newspapers publish per day? *The Atlantic.*

Barend Mons and Jan Velterop. 2009. Nano-publication in the e-science era. *Workshop on Semantic Web Applications in Scientific Discourse.*

Paul Rissen, Helen Lippell, Matt Chadburn, Tom Leitch, Dan Brickley, Michael Smethurst, and Sebastien Cevey. 2013. News storyline ontology.

Marco Rospocher, Marieke van Erp, Piek Vossen, Antske Fokkens, Itziar Aldabe, German Rigau, Aitor Soroa, Thomas Ploeger, and Tessel Bogaard. 2016. Building event-centric knowledge graphs from news. *Web Semantics: Science, Services and Agents on the World Wide Web*, 37:Pages 132–151.

Rolf Schwitter. 2010. Controlled natural languages for knowledge representation. *Proceedings of the 23rd International Conference on Computational Linguistics*, pages 1113–1121.

Stephanie Strassel, Dan Adams, Henry Goldberg, Jonathan Herr, Ron Keesing, Daniel Oblinger, Heather Simpson, Robert Schrag, and Jonathan Wright. 2010. The darpa machine reading program - encouraging linguistic and reasoning research with a series of reading tasks. In *Proceedings of the Seventh International Conference on Language Resources and Evaluation (LREC'10)*. European Language Resources Association (ELRA), may.

Kim Wedenberg and Alexander Sjberg. 2014. Online inference of topics: Implementation of lda topic modeling using an online variational bayes inference algorithm to sort news articles. Technical report, Uppsala Universitet, Uppsala, Sweden, February.

Gian Piero Zarri. 2009. *Representation and Management of Narrative Information*. Springer-Verlag, London, United Kingdom.

# Storyline detection and tracking using Dynamic Latent Dirichlet Allocation

**Daniel Brüggermann, Yannik Hermey, Carsten Orth,**
**Darius Schneider, Stefan Selzer, Gerasimos Spanakis** *
Department of Data Science and Knowledge Engineering
Maastricht University
Maastricht, Netherlands, 6200MD
{d.bruggermann, y.hermey, c.orth, d.schneider,
s.selzer, jerry.spanakis}@maastrichtuniversity.nl

## Abstract

In this paper we consider the problem of detecting and tracking storylines over time using news text corpora. World wide web creates vast amounts of information and handling, managing and utilizing this information is difficult without having systems that are able to identify trends, arcs and stories and how they evolve through time. The proposed approach utilizes a dynamic version of Latent Dirichlet Allocation (DLDA) over discrete time steps and makes it possible to identify topics within storylines as they appear and track them through time. Moreover, a graphical tool for visualizing topics and changes is implemented and allows for easy navigation through the topics and their corresponding documents. Experimental analysis on Reuters RCV1 corpus reveals that the proposed approach can be effectively used as a tool for identifying turning points in storylines and their evolutions while at the same time allowing for an efficient visualization.

## 1  Introduction

Growth of internet came along with an increasingly complex amount of text data from emails, news sources, forums, etc. As a consequence, it is impossible for individuals to keep track of all relevant storylines and moreover to detect changes in emerging trends or topics.

Many stakeholders (companies, individuals, policy makers, etc.) would be interested to harness the amount of free text data available in the web in order to develop intelligent algorithms that are able to react to emerging topics as fast as possible and at the same time track existing topics over long time spans. There are many techniques about topic extraction like Nonnegative Matrix Factorization (NMF) (Sra and Dhillon, 2005) or Latent Dirichlet Allocation (LDA) (Blei et al., 2003) but there are not many extensions to dynamic data handling. Time dependent modeling of documents can be computationally expensive and complex (Allan et al., 1998) and despite the fact that such approaches can be effective, none of these effectively handles the visualization issue which can make results more intuitive. Thus, effective approaches in terms of both computation and visualization of the results need to be pursued.

---

* Authors contributed equally to the manuscript, thus appear in alphabetical order. Correspondence to: jerry.spanakis@maastrichtuniversity.nl



*Proceedings of 2nd Workshop on Computing News Storylines*, pages 9–19,
Austin, TX, November 5, 2016. ©2016 Association for Computational Linguistics

This research work aims at implementing a technique to present stories and their changes from a news items flow by detecting and tracking topics through time. Results will be visualized and evaluated using the (fully annotated and immediately available) RCV1 Reuters corpus (810.000 documents) which is partly utilized in this work. The remainder of the paper is organized as follows. Section 2 presents an overview of current research work in the area. The proposed approach is described in Section 3, while experimental results are presented in Section 4. Finally, Section 5 concludes the paper and presents future improvement work.

## 2  Related Work

Topic detection and tracking is a long studied task (Fiscus and Doddington, 2002) and many approaches have already been attempted. Nonnegative matrix factorization is used in the field of text mining to factorize and thereby decrease the dimension of a large matrix (Lee and Seung, 1999). For topic detection, the original matrix can be composed of terms represented in the rows and documents represented in the columns, while the cell values represent the TF-IDF value (Sparck Jones, 1972) of each term in each document. As TF-IDF values cannot be negative, the algorithm's requirement of a matrix with only non-negative values is fulfilled. Ranking the terms of a topic by their matrix value reveals the most relevant terms that can make up the description of this topic. In a similar way, documents of a topic can be ranked as well. This makes it possible to visualize topics according to their importance amongst all documents (Godfrey et al., 2014).

There exist only few approaches so far that applied NMF for dynamically changing text data, i.e. when detecting and tracking topics

over time. Although the original data size can be too large for matrix factorization, there already exist variants of the algorithm using an dynamic approach, processing data in chunks (Wang et al., 2011). (Cao et al., 2007) use an online NMF algorithm that applies the factorization to the data of each time step and then updates the matrix bases from the previous calculations accordingly by some metric. However, both these algorithms are not able to detect emerging topics. (Saha and Sindhwani, 2012) defines an evolving set and an emerging set of topics within the NMF algorithm and appends the matrices accordingly in both dimensions whenever a new time step is considered. Topics are only detected when they emerge rapidly, and removing topics that are not relevant anymore is not discussed (the matrices increase gradually). (Tannenbaum et al., 2015) introduces a sliding window over the time steps. First, NMF is applied on a certain time step, and then the discovered topics are assigned to the topic model defined by the previous time steps, if possible. If they do not fit into the model, they are added to the emerging set of topics, which are added to the model as soon as there are enough documents that cover this new topic. Within the emerging set, the texts are categorized into new topics using hierarchical clustering.

All these works have several drawbacks. First, they mostly focus on sources like social media (Yang and Leskovec, 2011), (Paul and Girju, 2009), thus the magnitude of their data is several orders smaller than ours. Moreover, temporal dimension introduces further complexity due to the need for additional distributions or function that characterize this dynamic change (Hong et al., 2011).

Latent Dirichlet Allocation (LDA) (Blei et al., 2003) is a generative probabilistic mixture model for topic detection. In such a model, words define a vocabulary and topics are represented by a probabilistic distribution of words from this vocabulary. Each word may be part of several topic representations. LDA assumes that each document from a collection of documents is generated from a probabilistic distribution of topics. Bayes' Theorem in combination with a Dirichlet distribution as prior distribution are used to approximate the true posterior distribution. The probability space defined by the probabilities of the words and topics is multi-dimensional which is represented by a multinomial distribution. For the a priori estimation the conjugate distribution is needed, which corresponds to a Dirichlet distribution in this case. Information gain is used as measure for the difference between two iterated probability distributions and thereby acts as convergence criterion.

LDA has been extended in order to handle documents over long periods and many variations exist. Other approaches have been proposed as well (Banerjee and Basu, 2007) but scalability is an issue and visualization is not feasible. A milestone in the area was the work of (Wang and McCallum, 2006) since they associated a beta distribution over time with each topic to capture its popularity. There are also nonparametric models developed either using Gaussian mixture distributions (Ahmed and Xing, 2012) or utilizing Markovian assumptions (Dubey et al., 2013). These models are very effective but it is very difficult to choose a good distribution over time that allows both flexible changes and effective inferences. Disadvantage of these methods is that they either exhibit limited forms of temporal variation, or require computationally expensive inference methods.

There are extensions of the LDA model towards topic tracking over time such as (Wei et wards topic tracking over time such as (Wei et al., 2007). But according to (Wang et al., 2008), these methods deal with constant topics and the timestamps are used for better discovery. Opposed to that, our approach utilizes a dynamic model of LDA (Blei and Lafferty, 2006) that after examining the generated distributions for changes is able to detect turning points or storyline arcs. Finally, results are visualized using a stacked graph modeling and can be explored in an intuitive way by relating one topic to another.

LDA was selected due to the fact that topic modeling provides a powerful tool to uncover the thematic structure of large document collections. Moreover, the dynamic version of it (DLDA) offers the possibility of analyzing the topic distributions per time and provide insights on their changes and evolutions. Pre-selecting the number of topics is a known disadvantage of traditional LDA models, however experiments show that evolution of topics can still be identified between consecutive time steps. Selecting the initial number of topics relies on user requirements and on how much detail in the storylines (and their changes) is desired.

## 3 The proposed approach

### 3.1 Preprocessing

The preprocessing steps are separated into two major parts. First, the article text is extracted from the original documents and then the text is analyzed using natural language processing techniques to generate a meaningful vocabulary for the topic extraction. Then, the main natural language processing of the article text, namely the tokenization, named entity recognition (NER) and lemmatization, is performed using the Stanford CoreNLP (Manning et al., 2014). The text is split into single tokens and then these are filtered according to the categories, that the named entity recognition assigned to them. As numbers are not very descriptive for topics, the named entity recognition is used to exclude all tokens categorized in number-related categories, precisely those of the categories "DATE", "DURATION", "MONEY", "NUMBER", "ORDINAL", "PERCENT", "TIME" and "SET".

Lemmatization is used to normalize the tokens without loosing informational detail. Standard stemming algorithms aggressively reduce words to a common base even if these words are actually of different meaning thus they are not considered here (e.g. there is a difference between "marketing" and "markets"). On the other hand, lemmatization only removes inflectional endings and returns a dictionary form of the token.

The Stanford parser is highly context dependent and does not always categorize words correctly. As there are a lot of number-related words left, an additional step of removing such words is performed by regex-cleaning. This step also removes any words containing special characters human language words normally do not contain.

The next normalization step involves removing dashes and concatenating combined words as well as spell correction. As the news articles contain a lot of proper names and improperly resolving ambiguities can lead to loss of information, spell correction is done very carefully. The Levenshtein distance is used (Navarro, 2001) to correct those words of distance one who do not reveal ambiguities when compared to the entries of the official Hunspell dictionary. Named identities are excluded, as they cannot be correctly processed automatically. As the spell correction is computationally expensive, care is also taken, that it is only performed, when it makes sense. A preliminary, much faster test for existing equal words of the same length in the dictionary is preformed beforehand. A comparison is only done when the length of the strings differs by no more than the tested distance, which is 1 in this case. Last but not least, the spell correction is done as almost final step, after all the other refinements are applied.

Finally, the remaining list is filtered using a stopword list, that contains the most common words like "the" and "and". Such words do not contribute to reasonable meaning of the article and are not useful to identify topic content.

## 3.2 Dynamic Latent Dirichlet Allocation (DLDA)

The Dynamic LDA model is adopted and used on topics aggregated in time epochs and a state space model handles transitions of the topics from one epoch to another. A gaussian probabilistic model to obtain the posterior probabilities on the evolving topics along the time line is added as additional dimension. Figure 1 shows a graphical representation of the dynamic topic model.

DLDA (as LDA) needs to know the number of topics in advance. That depends on the user and the number of stories that we could like to be detected. For example, the RCV1 corpus has 103 actually used annotated topics, plus a large amount of unlabeled documents, so the parameter for the extraction is set to 104 topics. This corresponds to the 103 annotated topics and one additional "ERROR" topic for the unlabeled documents. Goal for this was to as accurately cover the original categories of the corpus, although more experiments with less topics (15, 30 and 60) were conducted. Moreover, the timestep has to be determined at this point. This again can be set to any time unit. For example, the RCV1 corpus used here (July and August of 1996) contains 42 days which makes exactly 6

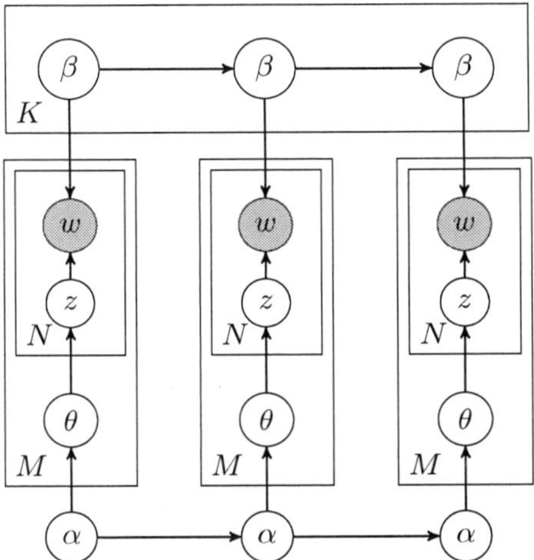

Figure 1: Plate diagram representing the dynamic topic model (for three time slices) as a Bayesian network. The model for each time slice corresponds to the original LDA process. Additionally, each topic's parameters $\alpha$ and $\beta$ evolve over time (Blei and Lafferty, 2006)

weeks of time. The dynamic topic model is accordingly applied to 6 time steps corresponding to the 6 weeks of the data set.

## 3.3 Topic emergence and storyline detection

DLDA produces a list of topic distributions per time step. Topics appear not to evolve in a great degree and this trend is reflected by the word distributions. Inspecting them in detail reveals little difference among the word distributions for the time steps of each topic. Figure 2 shows the word distribution scores for the time steps 0 and 1 and the difference between them for a topic from the RCV1 corpus. The number of topics in the dynamic topic model is fixed and the computation infers the topics through a probabilistic distribution. This does not produce dynamic topics (appearing or disappearing) but instead, the word distributions for one topic could be used to capture gradual changes gradually over time and detect a new turning point (or arc) in the storyline of this topic.

To identify such turning points and changes inside the word distributions, the second step of the two folded approach consists of applying a similarity measure to identify time steps, where the word distributions change enough to identify a new arc within current topic. Cosine similarity is used in this case to measure differences in the distributions from time step to time step.

$$diff_i = ||TD_i(t) - TD_i(t-1)|| \quad (1)$$

where:

- $i$ refers to current topic,

- $TD_i(t)$ refers to the topic distribution at current time-step $t$,

- $TD_i(t-1)$ refers to the topic distribution at previous time-step $t-1$

A turning point is identified if $diff_i$ is larger than a threshold which can be selected by the user (see next Section for more details on this). This is interpreted as a change to the topic distribution, which means that significant events within the topic are noticed, and add new information to the storyline. These changes in the storylines can also be visualized by a topic river like the one in Figure 3. Peaks (like for example the yellow peak at the 3rd time-step reveal important changes in the storyline development and thus can be used to monitor the storyline. It is therefore assumed that each topic corresponds to one storyline.

Moreover, storyline aggregation can be performed using the same similarity measure as before. Points of aggregation, where previously

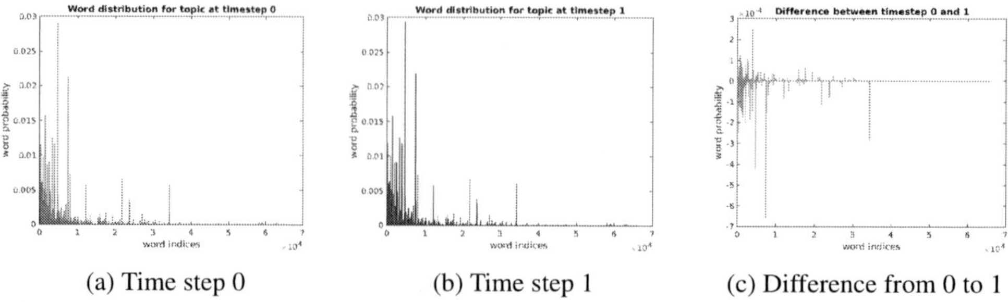

(a) Time step 0       (b) Time step 1       (c) Difference from 0 to 1

Figure 2: Example word distributions for neighboring time steps of one topic

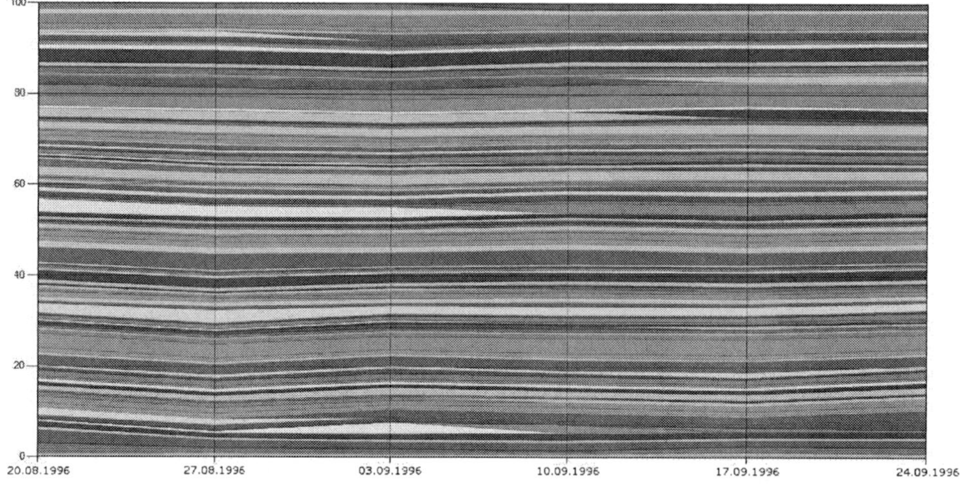

Figure 3: Topic rivers for August and September 1996 for emerging topics

separate topics should become one, are computed this way. As DLDA once more does a good job in clustering, the distance between different topics is rather high.

## 4 Experiments

### 4.1 The dataset

The process described in Section 3.1 is applied to the text content of the news articles from August and September 1996 of the RCV1 corpus (Lewis et al., 2004) to obtain a vocabulary containing terms, that are as meaningful and descriptive as possible while eliminating as much noise, consisting of not descriptive or ambiguous terms, as possible. The first two months of the RCV1 corpus contain 83.650 documents, which is about 10% of the corpus documents overall. Table 1 shows the results of the reduction of the number of terms from 308.854 distinct terms of about 16 million words overall to a final vocabulary size of 131.202.

Preprocessing leads to a reduction to 42% of the number of distinct tokens. Most important reduction in the vocabulary size comes from the NER category removals (almost half) which

14

| Overall terms | 16.467.261 | |
| --- | --- | --- |
| Distinct tokens | 308854 | 100.00% |
| NER category removals | 133976 | 43.38% |
| Lemmatization removals | 17372 | 5.62% |
| Regex cleanup removals | 18962 | 6.14% |
| Spellcheck cleanup removals | 6768 | 2.19% |
| Stopword removals | 574 | 0.19% |
| Final vocabulary size | 131202 | 42.48% |

Table 1: Terms and vocabulary for documents of August and September 1996 of RCV1

contributes most to keeping words and tokens that contribute most to the topics/storylines descriptions.

August and September 1996 contain newtimes from 42 days, thus 6 (weekly) timesteps are computed. Table 2 shows, that the documents are almost evenly distributed among the weeks.

| Aug 20th-26th | Aug 27th-Sep 2nd | Sep 3rd-9th | Sep 10th-16th | Sep 17th-23rd | Sep 24th-30th |
| --- | --- | --- | --- | --- | --- |
| 12807 | 12800 | 13953 | 14606 | 14487 | 14997 |

Table 2: Number of documents per week in August and September 1996 of RVC1

## 4.2 Storyline detection

The dynamic topic model partially identifies and reveals events of late summer 1996. Table 3 shows some of the identified events. The top 10 words of the topics' word distributions already give a precise overview of the topics' contents.

These topics describe events over a the period of two months and their change during the examined time frame (2 months) can be further explored in order to derive useful information for their evolution. This is done by comparing the topic distributions of consecutive weeks using Equation 1 and then turning points can be revealed if the following inequality is justified:

| Child abuse in Belgium | Tropical storm Edouard | Peace talks in Palestina | Kurdish war in Iraq |
| --- | --- | --- | --- |
| child | storm | israel | iraq |
| police | hurricane | peace | iraqi |
| woman | north | israeli | iran |
| death | wind | netanyahu | kurdish |
| family | west | minister | turkey |
| girl | mph | palestinian | northern |
| murder | mile | arafat | arbil |
| dutroux | coast | talk | baghdad |
| body | move | government | force |
| sex | flood | west | united |

Table 3: Extracted topics reveal events from August and September 1996

$$diff_i >= thres \qquad (2)$$

where $thres$ is a user-defined threshold which is set to the first quartile (Q1) (i.e. the middle number between the smallest and the median) of all $diff_i$ values for all topics $T$ at the first time step (i.e. $diff_i(1)$). This is justified due to the fact that depending on the corpus collection used, topic cohesion can vary from experiment to experiment. Other values were also tried (median, mean, 3rd quartile) but they proved to show very few changes in the storylines.

Table 4 shows the differences in the top 20 words of the word distributions for one example topic (about Iraq). Inspecting the top articles for this topic reveals an evolvement of the story behind the topic, as the main articles in the first weeks talk about the threat imposed by Iraqi forces and air strike battles, while the last weeks talk about concrete U.S. troop deployment in Kuwait. Table 5 presents the headlines of the corresponding articles for verification. While the first weeks the similarity between the distribution is almost identical (less than 0.01 difference), difference between week 3 and week 4 is significant (more than 0.02) and thus reflects this "turning point" within the same topic.

| week 1 | week 4 | week 5 |
|--------|--------|--------|
| iraq | iraq | iraq |
| missile | missile | gulf |
| attack | gulf | kuwait |
| saudi | iraqi | military |
| iraqi | military | missile |
| military | kuwait | iraqi |
| gulf | attack | united |
| force | united | force |
| united | force | saudi |
| war | zone | zone |
| defense | saddam | troops |
| air | defense | war |
| kuwait | war | attack |
| zone | saudi | defense |
| arab | air | washington |
| official | strike | arab |
| arabia | southern | official |
| strike | official | air |
| saddam | troops | saddam |
| southern | washington | arabia |

Table 4: Word distribution top word differences for Iraq topic

| week 1 - 3 | week 4 | week 5 - 6 |
|------------|--------|------------|
| Perry cites two incidents in Iraq no-fly zone. | Iraq fires at U.S. jets, U.S. bombers move closer. | U.S. boosts Kuwait defence by deploying Patriots. |
| U.S. warns it will protect pilots over Iraq. | U.S. gets Kuwaiti approval for troops deployment. | U.S. ground troops set to fly to Gulf. |
| Defiant Saddam urges his warplanes to resist U.S. | Kuwait agrees new troop U.S. deployment. | U.S. carrier enters Gulf, troops land in Kuwait. |
| Saddam urges his warplanes and gunners to resist. | Iraq says fired missiles at US and allied planes. | U.S. sends last of 3,000 ground troops to Gulf. |
| U.S. launches new attack on Iraq - officials. | Iraq fires at U.S. jets, U.S. bombers move closer. | U.S. declines to rule out Iraq strikes. |

Table 5: Article headlines for top documents of Iraq topic

Moreover, visualization works in a way that similar topics are on top of each other in the graph. Exploration of nearby topics can reveal further events within similar storylines. Table 6 shows the cosine similarity between two very similar topics (Iraq and Kurdish civil war) along the time line, while Table 7 gives an overview of the topic contents, represented by the top 20 words for each topic, at the time point with the highest similarity. The highest value for the cosine similarity, namely 0.613, can be found at time step 3 for two topics talking about the conflicts, the Iraq was involved in late 1996. Given these thresholds, both topics could be clustered further to a more general topic about Iraq politics, thus allowing for detecting the general storyline concept or the trend around these issues (if similarity threshold is high, then the current trend for these topics is low).

| week 1 | week 2 | week 3 | week 4 | week 5 | week 6 |
|--------|--------|--------|--------|--------|--------|
| 0.559 | 0.594 | 0.613 | 0.568 | 0.472 | 0.397 |

Table 6: Topic cosine similarities for both topics, Iraq and Kurdish Civil War, for each time step

| Iraq topic | Kurdish civil war topic |
|------------|-------------------------|
| iraq | iraq |
| missile | iraqi |
| attack | kurdish |
| iraqi | iran |
| military | northern |
| gulf | turkey |
| united | turkish |
| saddam | arbil |
| force | baghdad |
| zone | kdp |
| strike | united |
| kuwait | kurdistan |
| air | saddam |
| saudi | iranian |
| defense | puk |
| war | force |
| southern | official |
| baghdad | troops |
| action | border |
| official | kurds |

Table 7: Word distribution top word similarities for both topics, Iraq and Kurdish Civil War, at week 3

Finally, an example of some topics of summer 1996 and their presence (in terms of percentage of documents that the equivalent topic distribution is non-zero) is shown in Figure 4. One can identify topics that are recurring and present turning points (like the "Russia-1") which has two major hits or topics that have more bursty presence (like the "Olivetti" case in Italy or the "Tennis Open"). It should also be noticed the effect of topics that cover different stories under the same arc (e.g. the "plane crash" topics is already present in the news (referring mostly to TWA800 flight accident but it becomes more prevalent once a new plane crash in Russia (Vnukovo2801 flight) occurs, which also boosts the "Russia-1" since they are overlapping). These experiments reveal the ability of the system to identify turning points in storylines and track their presence and evolvement.

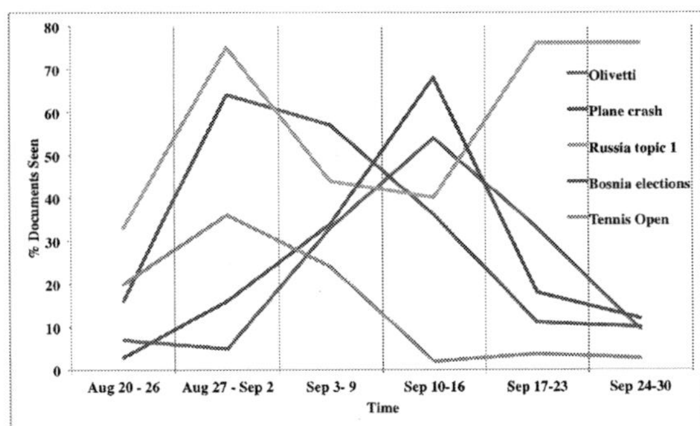


Figure 4: Emerging topics and turning points example

## 5    Discussion and Conclusion

This paper presented a Dynamic Latent Dirichlet Allocation for detecting storylines and monitor their development through time by revealing trends and similarities between evolved topics. The proposed approach was applied to news items of 6 weeks in August and September 1996 of the Reuters corpus RCV1. After applying careful preprocessing, it was possible to iden-

tify some of the main events happening at that time (e.g. the Kurdish civil war or the horrible crimes in Belgium). In order to identify details and possible turning points of a topic, a second step of comparing the word distributions inside each topic at each time step is added. Similarly, topics can also be aggregated revealing trends and arcs under the same storyline. Moreover, "burstiness" of topics can be detected and used for identifying new or recurring events.

Results from the RCV1 corpus subset reveal the possibilities of monitoring storylines and their evolvement through time and the opportunities for detecting turning points or identifying several sub-stories. Visualization of the results and the interaction with the stacked graph provide a framework for better monitoring the storylines. Further work involves the application of the model to the whole RCV1 corpus, as well as to the actual Reuters 2015 archive and develop a formal way to identify turning points and aggregate similar topics under a storyline. Moreover, evaluation of the output using human storyline evaluations will further improve model coherence and interpretation as well as validate the effect of the approach as to if identified storylines were correctly detected by the algorithm

# References

Amr Ahmed and Eric P Xing. 2012. Timeline: A dynamic hierarchical dirichlet process model for recovering birth/death and evolution of topics in text stream. *arXiv preprint arXiv:1203.3463*.

James Allan, Jaime G Carbonell, George Doddington, Jonathan Yamron, and Yiming Yang. 1998. Topic detection and tracking pilot study final report.

Arindam Banerjee and Sugato Basu. 2007. Topic models over text streams: A study of batch and online unsupervised learning. In *SDM*, volume 7, pages 437–442. SIAM.

David M. Blei and John D. Lafferty. 2006. Dynamic topic models. In *Proceedings of the 23rd International Conference on Machine Learning*, ICML '06, pages 113–120, New York, NY, USA. ACM.

David M. Blei, Andrew Y. Ng, and Michael I. Jordan. 2003. Latent dirichlet allocation. *J. Mach. Learn. Res.*, 3:993–1022, March.

Bin Cao, Dou Shen, Jian-Tao Sun, Xuanhui Wang, Qiang Yang, and Zheng Chen. 2007. Detect and track latent factors with online nonnegative matrix factorization. *IJCAI*, page 26892694.

Avinava Dubey, Ahmed Hefny, Sinead Williamson, and Eric P Xing. 2013. A nonparametric mixture model for topic modeling over time. In *SDM*, pages 530–538. SIAM.

Jonathan G. Fiscus and George R. Doddington. 2002. Topic detection and tracking. chapter Topic Detection and Tracking Evaluation Overview, pages 17–31. Kluwer Academic Publishers, Norwell, MA, USA.

Daniel Godfrey, Caley Johns, Carl Meyer, Shaina Race, and Carol Sadek. 2014. A case study in text mining: Interpreting twitter data from world cup tweets. *arXiv preprint arXiv:1408.5427*.

Liangjie Hong, Byron Dom, Siva Gurumurthy, and Kostas Tsioutsiouliklis. 2011. A time-dependent topic model for multiple text streams. In *Proceedings of the 17th ACM SIGKDD international conference on Knowledge discovery and data mining*, pages 832–840. ACM.

D. D. Lee and H. S. Seung. 1999. Learning the parts of objects by non-negative matrix factorization. *Nature*, page 788791.

David D. Lewis, Yiming Yang, Tony G. Rose, and Fan Li. 2004. RCV1: A New Benchmark Collection for Text Categorization Research. *J. Mach. Learn. Res.*, 5:361–397, December.

Christopher D. Manning, Mihai Surdeanu, John Bauer, Jenny Finkel, Steven J. Bethard, and David McClosky. 2014. The Stanford CoreNLP natural language processing toolkit. In *Association for Computational Linguistics (ACL) System Demonstrations*, pages 55–60.

Gonzalo Navarro. 2001. A guided tour to approximate string matching. *ACM Comput. Surv.*, 33(1):31–88, March.

Michael Paul and Roxana Girju. 2009. Cross-cultural analysis of blogs and forums with mixed-collection topic models. In *Proceedings of the 2009 Conference on Empirical Methods in Natural Language Processing: Volume 3-Volume 3*, pages 1408–1417. Association for Computational Linguistics.

Ankan Saha and Vikas Sindhwani. 2012. Learning evolving and emerging topics in social media: a dynamic nmf approach with temporal regularization. *Proceedings of the fifth ACM international conference on Web search and data mining*, page 693702.

Karen Sparck Jones. 1972. A statistical interpretation of term specificity and its application in retrieval. *Journal of documentation*, 28(1):11–21.

Suvrit Sra and Inderjit S Dhillon. 2005. Generalized nonnegative matrix approximations with bregman divergences. In *Advances in neural information processing systems*, pages 283–290.

Michael Tannenbaum, Andrej Fischer, and Johannes C. Scholtes. 2015. Dynamic Topic Detection and Tracking using Non-negative Matrix Factorization. In *Proceedings of the 27th Benelux Artificial Intelligence Conference (BNAIC)*. BNAIC.

Xuerui Wang and Andrew McCallum. 2006. Topics over time: a non-markov continuous-time model of topical trends. In *Proceedings of the 12th ACM SIGKDD international conference on*

*Knowledge discovery and data mining*, pages 424–433. ACM.

Chong Wang, David M. Blei, and David Heckerman. 2008. Continuous time dynamic topic models. In David A. McAllester and Petri Myllymki, editors, *UAI*, pages 579–586. AUAI Press.

Fei Wang, Ping Li, and Arnd Christian König. 2011. Efficient document clustering via online nonnegative matrix factorizations. In *SDM*, volume 11, pages 908–919. SIAM.

Xing Wei, Jimeng Sun, and Xuerui Wang. 2007. Dynamic mixture models for multiple time-series. In Manuela M. Veloso, editor, *IJCAI*, pages 2909–2914.

Jaewon Yang and Jure Leskovec. 2011. Patterns of temporal variation in online media. In *Proceedings of the fourth ACM international conference on Web search and data mining*, pages 177–186. ACM.

# Real-time News Story Detection and Tracking with Hashtags

**Gevorg Poghosyan** and **Georgiana Ifrim**
Insight Centre for Data Analytics
University College Dublin
Dublin, Ireland
{gevorg.poghosyan, georgiana.ifrim}@insight-centre.org

## Abstract

Topic Detection and Tracking (TDT) is an important research topic in data mining and information retrieval and has been explored for many years. Most of the studies have approached the problem from the event tracking point of view. We argue that the definition of stories as events is not reflecting the full picture. In this work we propose a story tracking method built on crowd-tagging in social media, where news articles are labeled with hashtags in real-time. The social tags act as rich meta-data for news articles, with the advantage that, if carefully employed, they can capture emerging concepts and address concept drift in a story. We present an approach for employing social tags for the purpose of story detection and tracking and show initial empirical results. We compare our method to classic keyword query retrieval and discuss an example of story tracking over time.

## 1 Introduction

We study the problem of automatically extracting and tracking[1] the storyline of news (i.e., the news articles covering the story events) for the purpose of improving the news presentation, both for consumption and research purposes (as targeted also in (Ahmed et al., 2011; Conrad and Bender, 2016; Leban et al., 2016)). Although this problem is widely addressed in the research literature from

machine learning, data mining and information retrieval communities, the issue of efficiently and effectively mapping large volumes of news articles to story timelines in real-time, remains challenging.

A news story often discusses multiple related events, which happen in different time periods and may as well involve different entities (people, countries, organisations). Some stories are relatively short in time, such as the 2016 Champions League final, and some others span many years and discuss multiple events, such as the Ebola outbreak or the migrant crisis. The story of the Syrian war, for example, has evolved in time, shifting the discussion **topic** (*Middle East, migration, human rights, politics*), the discussed **entities** (*Assad, ISIS, Putin, USA, Islamic State, Turkey, Hungary, Belgium*) and **events** (*rebel uprising, destruction of Syria's chemical weapons, Yazidi massacres, camerawoman kicking a migrant, liberation of Palmyra*). Figure 1 illustrates this drift in the projected topic-event-entity combined dimensions over time, in the news article space. The figure also shows that stories may share articles. For example, the article "Turkey carries out air strikes" may appear in several stories: *Syrian war, PKK in Syria, Turkey elections 2015*.

We propose to model story tracking as a real-time information retrieval problem. We assume to have access to a collection of news articles annotated with social tags extracted in real-time from social media platforms such as Twitter. This approach takes advantage of crowdsourced content as a form of real-time, continuous tagging of news. Additionally, social tags (aka hashtags)[2] are not necessarily topical:

---

[1] Corresponding to Topic Detection and Topic Tracking research applications defined by TDT community at http://www.itl.nist.gov/iad/mig/tests/tdt/

---

[2] The terms *social tag* and *hashtag* are used interchangeably in the



*Proceedings of 2nd Workshop on Computing News Storylines*, pages 20–29,
Austin, TX, November 5, 2016. ©2016 Association for Computational Linguistics

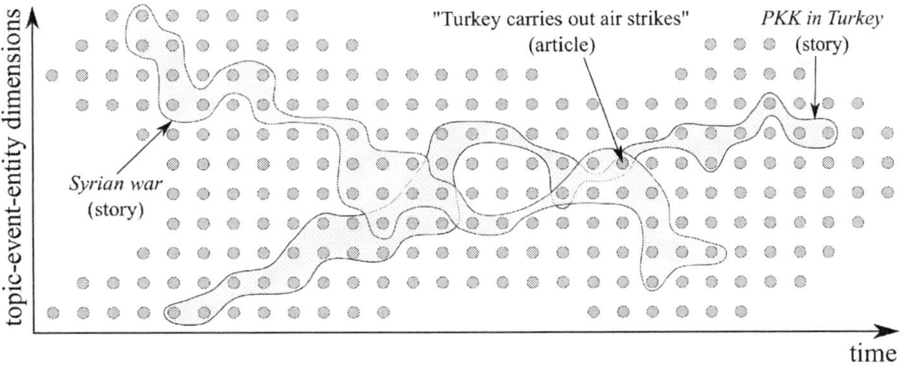


**Figure 1:** Stories' drift in topic-event-entity-time space.

they have the advantage of grouping together articles belonging to the same story (e.g., racial conflicts in US, #ericgarner, #blacklivesmatter, #icantbreathe) and allow the user to focus on diverse aspects of a story (e.g., Greek economic crisis, #grexit, #tsipras, #merkel, #ecb, #imf, #finland). We model a story as a query in an information retrieval framework where the query can mix keywords and hashtags.

From an application point of view, our work aims to automate the creation of story-focused pages and corresponding timelines, to enrich the storyline with context from social media (videos, tweets, posts, etc.) such as on `www.NewsDeeply.org` pages, and to provide story detection and tracking capabilities.

The choice of social tags is motivated by the following factors: (i) hashtags are inherently suitable for story tracking, as they are used on social platforms such as Twitter for tagging topics of interest[3], (ii) creation, popularity and abandonment of hashtags implicitly encode the concept drift in the story, (iii) hashtags allow cross-platform multi-modal content linking (text, image, video), (iv) tagging articles imposes no structural limitations for organising news as in single-linkage clustering (Ahmed et al., 2011; Conrad and Bender, 2016; Hou et al., 2015; Leban et al., 2016; Pouliquen et al., 2008). This approach is also consistent with trends in media: (a) social media oriented news providers like *AJ+* have embraced the usage of manually assigned

hashtags to organise their content, (b) both *The Guardian*[4] and *The Huffington Post*[5] are giving importance to hashtags by writing articles about the popular social tags and informing the public on discussion trends, (c) *The Sun* had published a newspaper with a hashtag[6] alongside an article[7].

By including hashtags in the query we can facilitate better query formulation, and therefore a better story tracking process. For example, searching for *#rmucl* (the hashtag for Real Madrid's UEFA Champions League (UCL) season) can help to narrow the search down to Real Madrid's solely UCL games (i) even if the articles do not contain any of the keywords (e.g., an article titled *"Zidane's squad beats Manchester City 1:0 (video)"* may have a short body not containing any of the search keywords), (ii) avoiding the noise from the Club's activities in the Spanish League (with dedicated hashtag *#rmliga*). The method implicitly allows the choice of story granularity and navigation to substories. Contrary to the *#rmucl* example, some hashtags, e.g., *#rip*, can also group articles about unrelated events and entities in a non-topical fashion.

The remainder of this paper is structured as follows. Section 2 describes the related work. In Section 3 we briefly introduce the notation used in the paper and the problem setup. Section 4 describes our approach for story detection and organizing the news

---

paper.

[3]http://www.nytimes.com/2011/06/12/fashion/hashtags-a-new-way-for-tweets-cultural-studies.html

[4]www.theguardian.com/technology/hashtags

[5]www.huffingtonpost.com/news/hashtags/

[6]www.huffingtonpost.com/2014/03/26/sun-hashtag-newspaper-murdoch-british_n_5034639.html

[7]"By printing hashtags alongside our news we are making it easy for readers to share their opinions and continue the story online," Sun editor David Dinsmore said in a statement

articles into stories. Section 5 explains our proposed method for story tracking. In Section 6 we present the evaluation of the proposed method, and, in Section 7 we conclude the paper and discuss future research.

## 2   Related Work

In this section we present related research spanning different research communities.

**Event detection and tracking:** Work presented by (Allan et al., 1998) tracks 25 predefined events, processing the articles in chronological order and making a binary decision on event relatedness for each article, before processing any subsequent articles. An assumption is made that each article discusses a single event. (Brown, 2001) provides an extension to (Allan et al., 1998) for real-time event detection. (Kuzey and Weikum, 2014) describe an offline system for populating event classes of knowledge bases by first mapping news to *Wikipedia* categories, then mapping the latter to WordNet event classes. (Leban et al., 2016) have designed a real-time system which groups articles about an event across languages. Articles are clustered based on their cosine similarity. An event is registered after a cluster reaches a certain size, whereas the cluster will be removed when it becomes older than 5 days.

**Tracking stories:** (Navrat et al., 2009) propose a system with a focused crawler which works on the user side and tracks a story by smartly selecting the links on the article page. The performance on the experimental set was noisy and the system purely relies on the existing links on the page. In the *European Media Monitor* from (Pouliquen et al., 2008) news articles are clustered using an agglomerative clustering algorithm. Stories are formed from clusters linked based on their cosine similarity. The system introduced in (Hou et al., 2015) represents each news article in the dimensions of entities, topics and events. A knowledge base is used for linking topics and linking entities and thus creating links between the articles. For a given query, a list of articles is returned ranked by the weighted sum of relevance and topic scores. (Ahmed et al., 2011) model news storyline clustering by applying a topic model to the clusters, while simultaneously generating single-linkage clusters using the Recurrent Chinese Restaurant Process. This approach allows the number of stories to be determined by the data. The system accuracy is evaluated on 2,525 manually judged "must-link" and "cannot-link" article pairs. (Conrad and Bender, 2016) have designed an event-centric hierarchical agglomerative clustering algorithm operating in real-time for providing a news browsing experience in a structured way, given the editorially supplied top-level story labels. *MediaMeter* introduced in (Nomoto, 2015) uses a tagger called *WikiLabel* for assigning Wikipedia labels to news articles and detects trending topics based on labels with high burstiness scores. (Vossen et al., 2015) discuss a framework for structuring massive news streams into storylines. The authors discuss a computational model of storylines and guidelines for storyline evaluation, but no comprehensive empirical study is presented.

**Query expansion:** (Verberne et al., 2016) studied query term suggestions for Boolean queries in a news monitoring system. They found that the premise of 'pseudo-relevance' does not hold for Boolean retrieval when the set of retrieved documents is noisy. (Anagnostopoulos et al., 2012) introduced a query expansion algorithm based on a semantic network of Twitter hashtags. They have shown that the social intelligence can be used to describe information and successfully applied it in query expansion.

**Contribution:** State-of-the-art systems rely on keyword/semantic matching and require often slow-to-change offline snapshots of knowledge bases (Kuzey and Weikum, 2014) or need computationally expensive, complex clustering or semantic models, where parameters such as the number of topics (Hou et al., 2015), timespan of stories (Conrad and Bender, 2016; Leban et al., 2016) and cluster sizes (Pouliquen et al., 2008), significantly affect the system performance.

Unlike the methods described above, we model storyline extraction as a pattern mining and real-time retrieval problem based on social annotations of news articles. The proposed approach has the following advantages which are important for our problem: (i) it is non-parametric over stories, allowing any size, duration, number of events, number of named entities, etc., (ii) stories are not bounded to predefined topics or taxonomies and the choice of query hashtags allows "zooming in" to substories, (iii) articles can be shared between storylines, so articles relevant to multiple stories can appear in each, not penalizing the recall of either story, (iv) no reliance on information from external knowledge bases, which may lag behind the relevant events, (v) the story will track the emerging as well as deprecating concepts (in the form of hashtags or keywords) relevant to the story, (vi) real-time performance is achieved without limiting the story size in articles or span in time, and without a need for recomputing any clusters or semantic models when new data arrives.

## 3   Preliminaries and Basic Notation

We assume to have a dataset of articles with recommended hashtags. The social tags can be manually assigned to an article by a journalist or by an automated hashtag recommender. *Hashtagger* presented in (Shi et al., 2016) and the method proposed in (Efron, 2010) recommend hashtags to news articles. We build on top of Hashtagger, which recommends up to 10 hashtags to an article, which are updated every 15 minutes over a period of 24 hours from the article publication time.

The notations used in this paper are summarized in Table 1. An article $Article_j$ may get up to $10 \times 24\,hours \times 4\,per\,hour = 960$ unique hashtags denoted as $\#tag_1^j \dots \#tag_{960}^j$, each recommended with a confidence[8] $conf_t^j \in [0.5, 1]$, where $0 < t \leqslant 960$. A single hashtag can be recommended to the same article with different confidences at different points in time. A query for story retrieval and tracking is composed of keywords $w_1, ..., w_n$ and hashtags $\#tag_1^q, ..., \#tag_m^q$, where $n + m > 0$. Each query also includes a time period from which the articles will be retrieved. We denote articles retrieved by query expansion by the superscript $^{ex}$. The retrieval score of $Article_j^{ex}$ is denoted as $score_j$.

We use the terms *substory* and *superstory* to refer to stories correspondingly narrower or wider in scope, than the reference story.

---

<sup></sup>[8]Manually assigned hashtags can get confidence set to 1 if no value is given.

| | |
|---|---|
| $n$ | number of terms in query |
| $m$ | number of hashtags in query |
| $q$ | query, where $n + m > 0$ |
| $p$ | number of full months in the query time period |
| $w_i$ | $i^{th}$ keyword in the query $q$, where $0 < i \leqslant n$ |
| $\#tag_i^q$ | $i^{th}$ hashtag in the query $q$, where $0 < i \leqslant m$ |
| $Article_j$ | the $j^{th}$ article in the database |
| $\#tag_t^j$ | $t^{th}$ hashtag recommended to $Article_j$, where $0 < t \leqslant 960$ |
| $conf_t^j$ | recommendation confidence of $\#tag_t^j$, where $0 < t \leqslant 960$ |
| $Article_j^{ex}$ | the $j^{th}$ article retrieved for query expansion, where $0 < j \leqslant 10+p$ |
| $score_j$ | retrieval score of the $j^{th}$ article retrieved for query expansion |
| $b$ | number of hashtag confidence bins |
| $k$ | number of highest score confidence bins, where $k \leqslant b$ |
| $\#tag_i$ | $i^{th}$ hashtag in the query expansion hashtag set |
| $score_{\#tag_i}$ | score assigned to $\#tag_i$ |
| $l$ | number of story expansion hashtags, where $l \leqslant 10+p$ |
| $M$ | number of articles retrieved with the expanded query |

**Table 1:** Notation used in the paper.

## 4   Story Detection via Frequent Hashtag Set Mining

We propose a method that maps news articles to stories in real-time, by grouping the articles with connected events, entities and topics that are discussed together on social platforms like Twitter. We use Twitter hashtags to group the news into stories. Each hashtag represents a story (e.g., *#turkey* or *#syria*) and a combination of hashtags represents a substory for each of the stories it is part of, e.g., {*#turkey, #syria*} represents the story of Turkish involvement in Syrian war.

### 4.1   Story Detection

This section describes a method for story detection using frequent pattern mining over hashtags.

A single news article can be covering multiple stories (Vossen et al., 2015) and some other articles can cover either a substory or a superstory of a story covered in the first article. We have observed that multiple articles covering the same story get assigned the same set of hashtags. We exploit this phenomenon to detect popular news stories by mining frequent hashtag sets which are being assigned to the same set of articles. Each frequent hashtag set (e.g., {*#turkey, #syria, #kurdistan*}), which is a superset of another hashtag set (e.g., {*#turkey, #syria*}), is a popular story too and is a substory of the story represented by the hashtag superset. This representation enables us to use the hierarchical structure of the story coverage for better navigation in the huge sea of stories.

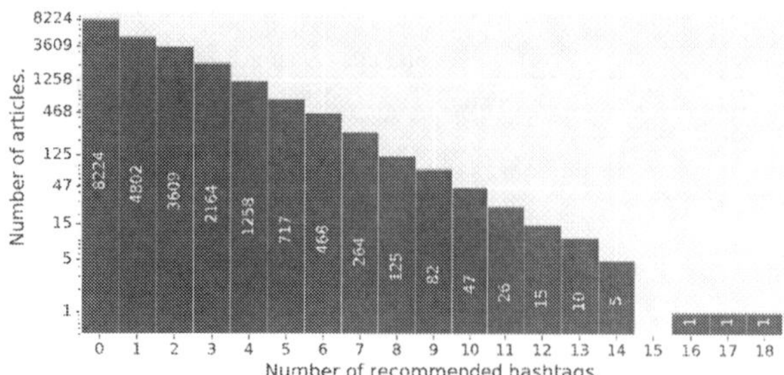

**Figure 2:** Distribution of number of recommended hashtags per article in the full set of all 21,819 articles from May 2016. 13,595 articles have at least one recommended hashtag with an average of 2.55 hashtags per article. 13,270 articles have at least one non-spammy recommended hashtag.

To study the possible advantages of the chosen representation, we run an experiment on a subset of 13,270 articles[9] from May 2016 (which represent 60.8% of all articles in this period) that have been linked to at least one hashtag. Overall 5,107 unique hashtags were recommended to the articles in May 2016. The histogram of number of recommended hashtags per article is shown in Figure 2. We have defined the articles as a support domain and have extracted frequent hashtag patterns co-occurring for a large number of articles.

We use an implementation of ECLAT[10] (Zaki, 2000) for mining the frequent hashtag sets. Running the ECLAT algorithm with a minimum support requirement[11] of 5 articles resulted in 6,839 frequent hashtag patterns of a form shown in Table 2. For example, the third line in Table 2 shows that there are 35 articles which got both {*#farewellboleyn*, *#whufc*} hashtags recommended to them.

The extracted patterns give an overview of all the topics covered in the news article set. In the following section we discuss how a user can navigate the big set of hashtag patterns which define detected stories.

| Pattern | Support |
| --- | --- |
| *#mufc* | 758 |
| *#trumptrain*　*#makeamericagreatagain* *#trump #trump*2016 | 59 |
| *#farewellboleyn #whufc* | 35 |

**Table 2:** Example frequent hashtag patterns mined from news articles in May 2016.

## 4.2 Hierarchical Story Representation

Visualization of mined stories can be done in many ways allowing navigation through the stories. The essential factors that have influenced our choice of visualization are: (i) the hierarchical structure of substory-superstory relationship must be shown, (ii) the user must be able to zoom in to substories, (iii) a substory can be navigated to from either of its superstories[12].

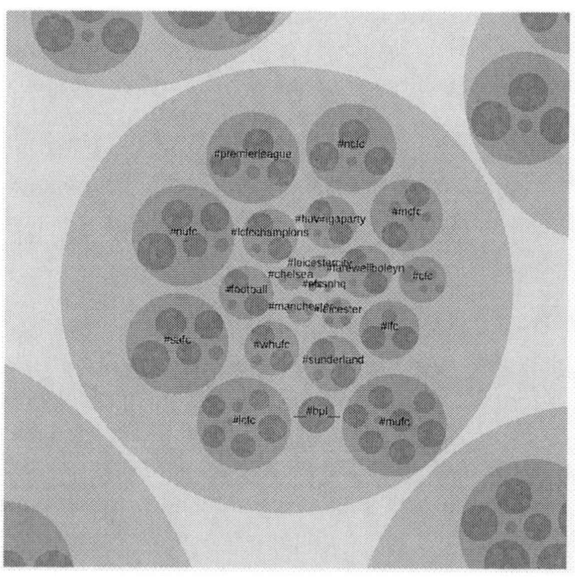

**Figure 3:** Screenshot of Barclays Premier League, aka #bpl story visualized.

We have used Zoomable Circle Packing[13] interactive visualization from D3 library[14] to visualize the stories. Figure 3 shows the *#bpl* story of Barclays Premier League of soccer. The inner blue bubbles represent the substories of *#bpl* and each includes a specific football club hashtag (e.g., *#mufc* for

---

[9]We filter out the recommendations of spammy hashtags which don't contribute to any certain story: #news, #business, #breaking, #politics, #jobs, #world, #rt, #sport, #breakingnews #follow.

[10]http://www.borgelt.net/eclat.html

[11]The support threshold can be varied to change the extracted set of patterns.

[12]This results in duplication of substories under each existing superstory.

[13]http://bl.ocks.org/mbostock/7607535

[14]http://github.com/d3/d3/wiki/Gallery

Manchester United football club). In this form of visualization, the {*#bpl*, *#mufc*} substory can be navigated from either *#bpl* or *#mufc* story. This choice results in duplicated data but keeps the strictly hierarchical structure of news stories.

The interactive visualization of May 2016 stories and the corresponding data are available online[15].

In contrast to related work, this pattern set structure allows us to represent the news in a hierarchical, multiple-linkage browsable structure, where one can "zoom in" into a multi-hashtag substory while, at the same time, allowing a hashtag (and articles linked to it) to be a part of another story. The frequent sets can be maintained and updated upon the fresh data arrival or alternatively mined again in a periodic fashion (e.g., once an hour).

## 5  Story Tracking via Retrieval with Social Tags

In the previous section we discussed how to detect stories from article-hashtag sets. We now formulate *story tracking* as a retrieval task with queries that allow mixing of keywords and hashtags. This allows tracking stories on-the-fly rather than being restricted to a pre-determined set of stories. We represent an article by its headline, subheadline, body, a set of summary keywords and a set of hashtags recommended to the article. The recommended hashtags are binned into $b = 20$ confidence bins with ranges from $(0.975, 1.0]$, down to $(0.5, 0.525]$ and indexed to enable an efficient search on article fields with different weighting using the BM25 algorithm (Robertson et al., 1994). The retrieval is done with the following settings:

- Keywords $w_1, ..., w_n$ are matched on article keywords, headline, subheadline and content with score boost of correspondingly $\times 4$, $\times 3$, $\times 2$ and $\times 1$. The idea behind this weighting is that an article matching a query in its headline, is more likely to belong to the requested story, rather than in the case when the matching keywords appear somewhere in the article body.

- Hashtags $\#tag_1^q, ..., \#tag_m^q$ are matched on the top-$k$ hashtag confidence bins with score boosting of $6 - \frac{(i+1) \times 2}{b}$ for a match on bin $0 < i \leqslant k$.



The idea behind the decaying per bin boost is that more confidently recommended hashtags are more likely to be relevant to the story.

Figure 4 gives an overview of the proposed method. To retrieve the articles covering a certain story, we do a two-step retrieval in the given time period by expanding the original query in the "hashtag space", then retrieving the story articles with the expanded query. The step-by-step process is the following:

1. To get a set of potentially relevant to the story hashtags, we use the recommended hashtags of the top-$(10+p)$ articles (shown as $Article_j^{ex}$ on Figure 4) from the initial search results, where $p$ is the number of full months in the queried time period. The intuition behind the parameter $p$ is that longer stories would possibly include more events, entities and topics and presumably these may be covered in more articles. On the other hand, using too many articles for the query expansion is bound to introduce more noise. Among the top-$(10 + p)$ articles, we only use for query expansion those whose $score_j \geqslant 0.5 \times score_1$, i.e., the matching score is not lower than 50% of the top match article score. This approach allows to narrow down to the more focused story when an overlap of coverage exists between the query terms.

2. The query expansion hashtags are chosen from the set of hashtags recommended to any of the $10+p$ articles. Because the same hashtag may be recommended to several of chosen $10+p$ articles, we first weight hashtags by the product of their recommendation confidence to an article and the article matching score on the query, and then we take the highest of these scores for a given hashtag. Hashtags of the filtered set of articles are weighted by the following formula:

$$score_{\#tag_i} = max_{1 < j \leqslant 10+p,\ \#tag_i = \#tag_r^j}(score_j \times conf_r^j)$$

where $score_j$ is the matching score of the $j^{th}$ article from $(10 + p)$ retrieved articles, $tag_r^j$ is the $r^{th}$ recommended hashtag with confidence $conf_r^j$ for the article $Article_j^{ex}$. The resulting set is limited to $(10 + p)$ unique hashtags with the highest scores $score_{\#tag_i}$, where $0 < i \leqslant (10+p)$, that will serve as a query expansion set of hashtags, denoted as $\#tag_1, ..., \#tag_l$ on

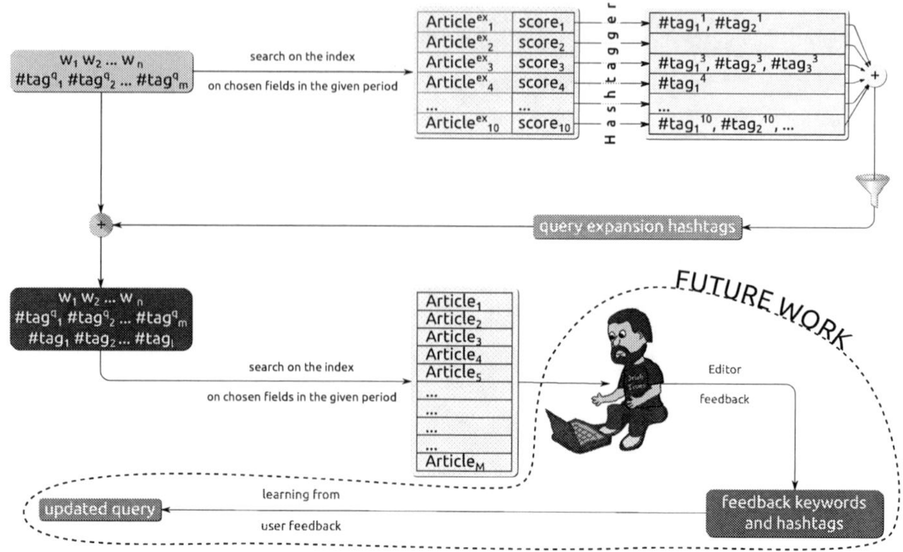


**Figure 4:** Story retrieval process diagram.

Figure 4. The initial query together with the query expansion hashtags form what we call the story tracking query.

3. A second retrieval using the expanded query, returns the final set of ranked articles $Article_1, ..., Article_M$. The method works even for cases where there are no hashtags recommended to an article, but the presence of hashtags allows for more refined queries.

The hyper-parameters of the system, like the query boosting parameters, $b$, $k$, as well as the heuristic methods like the choice of $10+p$ articles are yet not fully evaluated, and the used values were chosen empirically.

The stories can be tracked by simply re-initiating the whole process described in Figure 4 at anytime. A fresh retrieval, i.e., re-issuing the same query, allows to (i) capture the previously unseen events and entities covered in newly arrived articles, (ii) capture emerging relevant story hashtags in the query expansion, (iii) retrieve currently relevant articles, which might not be matching the previously used query. Hashtags once present in the query expansion, will remain in the story defining query to ensure the completeness of story coverage.

## 6 Evaluation

We have been tracking 27 RSS news feeds from 8 (mostly Irish[16]) news organisations, starting from August 2015. This allows us to track stories that have started capturing the public attention almost a year ago. A side effect of our news selection is that the social content, and therefore also the hashtags that are linked to articles, are biased towards Ireland-related issues.

For a preliminary evaluation of our method we compare the performance of article retrieval with the expanded query to a retrieval with the initial input query in identical setup. To show the effect of query expansion hashtags, we also include in the evaluation a retrieval with expansion hashtags only. The evaluation is performed on the following 5 queries: *migrant crisis*, *refugee crisis*, *US election*, *EURO 2016* and *#euro2016*. Many news providers offer story-focused pages with curated collections of news articles. We select news articles from The Irish Times story-pages as a ground truth for each story[17].

---

[16]*The Irish Times, The Irish Independent, RTÉ, TheJournal.ie, Irish Examiner, BBC, Reuters* and *Al Jazeera*

[17]The URLs of the curated story pages corresponding to our selected 5 queries are:
http://www.irishtimes.com/news/world/europe/migrant-crisis
http://www.irishtimes.com/news/world/us/us-election
http://www.irishtimes.com/sport/euro-2016

The curated story-pages serve as a natural ground truth for evaluating our story extraction, because our method aims to automate the creation of this kind of pages. There are only few active curated story-pages on news platforms, which limits our ground truth collection and is the main reason behind our choice of queries. For the purpose of evaluation, we correspondingly limit the retrieval from the database to The Irish Times articles from the time period covered by the curated story page. Our goal is not necessarily to evaluate the retrieval quality, but to show that the social tags can improve the story extraction. Table 3 presents the evaluation metrics including the Recall and NDCG@k as defined in (Manning et al., 2008). NDCG@k reflects the quality of ranking, and in our case shows how similar our stories are to those on curated story pages.

| Query | Query expansion hashtags | Time period | Number of articles on the curated page and in our database | Match | Articles | Recall | NDCG @10 | NDCG @25 |
|---|---|---|---|---|---|---|---|---|
| migrant crisis | #lybia #pope #popefrancis #eu #health #migrants #greece #turkey #utah #lesbos #italy #francis | 07 Apr - 14 Jun | 45 | initial query | 782 | 88.9% | 0.2083 | 0.2549 |
| | | | | expansion hashtags only | 294 | 46.7% | 0.2903 | 0.2449 |
| | | | | expanded query | 984 | 91.1% | 0.3398 | 0.3565 |
| refugee crisis | #refugees #bono #eu #turkey #un #refugee #china | 07 Apr - 14 Jun | 45 | initial query | 783 | 84.4% | 0.6204 | 0.3896 |
| | | | | expansion hashtags only | 244 | 28.9% | 0.2201 | 0.1741 |
| | | | | expanded query | 964 | 88.9% | 0.5321 | 0.3819 |
| US election | #modiinus #hillaryclinton #deleteyouraccount #peru #freedom #primaryday #eu #imwithher #modifiedforeignpolicy #kuczynski #hillary | 06 Jun - 15 Jun | 19 | initial query | 516 | 94.7% | 0.2248 | 0.2424 |
| | | | | expansion hashtags only | 31 | 36.8% | 0.3909 | 0.2971 |
| | | | | expanded query | 524 | 94.7% | 0.4748 | 0.3420 |
| EURO 2016 | #euro2016 | 30 May - 15 Jun | 12 | initial query | 572 | 83.3% | 0 | 0 |
| | | | | expansion hashtags only | 155 | 41.7% | 0 | 0.0607 |
| | | | | expanded query | 604 | 100% | 0 | 0.0293 |
| #euro2016 | #romania #england #wal #eng #russia #marseille | 30 May - 15 Jun | 12 | initial query | 155 | 41.7% | 0 | 0.0607 |
| | | | | expansion hashtags only | 165 | 41.7% | 0 | 0.0252 |
| | | | | expanded query | 165 | 41.7% | 0 | 0.0252 |

**Table 3:** Evaluation results.

Table 3 shows that the query expansion does not contribute dramatically to Recall. However for *migrant crisis* and *US election* stories, the improvement in NDCG is significant. The *refugee crisis* story is a good example for demonstrating the sensitivity of the query expansion as the evaluation for it was done on the same ground truth curated page as for the *migrant crisis*. Also one can notice the presence of #bono[18] in the query expansion set. Bono has several times visited refugee camps and spoken

for the rights of migrants. Nevertheless the importance and relatedness of #bono to the story is slightly overshadowed by a significant coverage about Bono in our news corpus of mostly Irish sources. Querying *EURO 2016*, although successfully expands the query with the relevant hashtag, retrieves noisy results. The performance figures can be explained by the high ambiguity of the query, as *EURO* may refer to the currency or politics. Regardless of the unimpressive performance metrics for the latter query, the takeaway point is that the ambiguity problem can be solved by issuing a query *#euro2016* instead, and this is one of the key features of our method, offered as a solution to the ambiguity problem.

The live system used in the experiments for evaluation is described in our previous work (Poghosyan et al., 2016) and is available online[19].

**Story Tracking and Concept Drift:** In Table 4 we show the query expansion hashtags for the *migrant crisis* story for each two weeks from January 1st to May 31st 2016, to illustrate the potential of hashtags to track a story with the proposed method. It can be noticed that the query expansion has successfully captured the newly emerged entities in the story. Methods relying on offline knowledge bases may not be responsive enough to capture the new relationships of entities in stories.

| Period (2016) | Query expansion hashtags for the query *migrant crisis* |
|---|---|
| Jan 1 - Jan 15 | #migrantcrisis #crisis #migrant |
| Jan 1 - Jan 31 | #migrant #germany #calais #corbyn |
| Jan 1 - Feb 15 | #calais #corbyn #germany #migrant |
| Jan 1 - Feb 29 | #calais #greece #migrant #corbyn #germany #refugees |
| Jan 1 - Mar 15 | #calais #migrants #macedonia #greece #turkey #migrant #corbyn #germany #refugees #eu |
| Jan 1 - Mar 31 | #calais #migrants #macedonia #greece #turkey #migrant #corbyn #germany #refugees #eu |
| Jan 1 - Apr 15 | #calais #migrants #macedonia #greece #turkey #migrant #corbyn #germany #refugees #eu |
| Jan 1 - Apr 30 | #calais #migrants #macedonia #greece #turkey #migrant #corbyn #germany #refugees #lesbos #eu |
| Jan 1 - May 15 | #calais #migrants #macedonia #greece #turkey #migrant #corbyn #germany #refugees #lesbos #eu |
| Jan 1 - May 31 | #calais #migrants #macedonia #greece #turkey #migrant #corbyn #germany #refugees #lesbos #eu |

**Table 4:** Example of the expanded query evolution in time for the query *migrant crisis*.

---

[18]Bono is an Irish musician best known as the lead vocalist of rock band U2

[19]http://lovelace.ucd.ie/tutorial_video

# 7 Conclusions and Future Work

In summary, we propose a new angle on story detection and tracking based on frequent pattern mining and real-time retrieval of tagged news articles. To the best of our knowledge there is no other method which exploits real-time hashtag recommendations for this purpose. We present a frequent pattern-based story detection which allows "zooming in/out" into substories and superstories. The advantage of our proposed story tracking solution is that it quickly adapts to emerging entities or events and their relatedness, because it does not require a slow-to-change knowledge base. Our solution is real-time and does a retrieval on-demand without the need of recomputing any clusters or semantic models when new data arrives. The weaknesses of our story tracking approach include the strong reliance on the hashtag recommender (although Hashtagger has 85% Precision@1) and the potential lack of story discussions on social platforms, e.g., Hashtagger recommends at least 1 hashtag to about 65% of all articles. This can be mitigated to some extent possibly by expanding our scope to other social platforms that increasingly adopt social tags. Yet another workaround for compensating for the partial hashtag coverage is discussed below in the future work.

**Future Work.** We intend to have a deeper evaluation of the story detection and tracking by expanding the experiments to multiple news sources and a larger set of stories. We also consider necessary to perform an evaluation involving manual annotation of the retrieved articles by a domain expert. The heuristic elements of the method have an intuition behind and are set only empirically. These elements require an evaluation of their contribution.

We believe a more accurate query expansion with weighted hashtags will allow to distinguish the stories which have the same set of linked hashtags, but different dominant hashtags. Weighted queries will also enable the automation of query updates for story tracking and incorporation of human feedback for refining the query over time.

The query formulation largely affects both the query expansion and subsequently also the final article retrieval (as we have shown in Section 6). The task of composing good queries is not trivial and an exploration of a substory may not be achieved only by modifying the query. For this reason a user feedback loop may be added to allow the query issuer to steer the story in the desired direction (see Figure 4).

The issue of diversity of news articles within a retrieved (and possibly curated) story is also interesting. We plan on studying the literature on aspect-based information retrieval (Santos et al., 2010), where the hashtags would serve as natural aspects in our framework.

To compensate for the partial hashtag coverage of articles (60.8% for May 2016), the keywords extracted from the articles, along with the assigned hashtags, can be included in frequent pattern mining for story detection. This may significantly change the mined stories, as the tag space density and subsequently the mined patterns' cardinality may change.

Along with simple market basket type analysis to discover frequent subsets of hashtags linked to sets of articles, we plan to extend the storyline organization with including new dimensions like the source and the time. $n$-ary frequent pattern mining techniques like the one described in (Cerf, 2010) can extract patterns of form $\{source_1, ..., source_i \times month_1, ..., month_j \times \#tag_1, ..., \#tag_k\}$ which will help to analyze the temporal-topical patterns of sources and how these patterns are similar or different between the sources. We plan to explore the frequent patterns of hashtags linked to the articles of a source, to possibly discover the response of the audience using a similar vocabulary to the one of the source. We are also interested in news coverage comparison between the sources for different given stories with patterns of form $\{source_1, ..., source_i \times \#tag_1, ..., \#tag_k\}$.

Finally we plan to build on the story tracking method to automate story timeline and summary generation, similar to the ones found on www.NewsDeeply.org or The Irish Times curated pages.

# Acknowledgments

This work was funded by Science Foundation Ireland (SFI) under grant number 12/RC/2289.

# References

Amr Ahmed, Qirong Ho, Choon H Teo, Jacob Eisenstein, Eric P Xing, and Alex J Smola. 2011. Online inference for the infinite topic-cluster model: Storylines from streaming text. In *International Conference on Artificial Intelligence and Statistics*, pages 101–109.

James Allan, Jaime G Carbonell, George Doddington, Jonathan Yamron, and Yiming Yang. 1998. Topic detection and tracking pilot study final report.

Ioannis Anagnostopoulos, Vassilis Kolias, and Phivos Mylonas. 2012. Socio-semantic query expansion using twitter hashtags. In *SMAP*.

Ralf D Brown. 2001. A server for real-time event tracking in news. In *Proceedings of the first international conference on Human language technology research*, pages 1–3.

Loïc Cerf. 2010. *Constraint-based mining of closed patterns in noisy n-ary relations*. Ph.D. thesis, INSA de Lyon.

Jack G. Conrad and Michael Bender. 2016. Semi-supervised events clustering in news retrieval. In *ECIR*.

Miles Efron. 2010. Hashtag retrieval in a microblogging environment. In *SIGIR*.

Lei Hou, Juanzi Li, Zhichun Wang, Jie Tang, Peng Zhang, Ruibing Yang, and Qian Zheng. 2015. News-miner: Multifaceted news analysis for event search. *Knowledge-Based Systems*, 76:17–29.

Erdal Kuzey and Gerhard Weikum. 2014. Evin: Building a knowledge base of events. In *WWW*, pages 103–106.

Gregor Leban, Blaz Fortuna, and Marko Grobelnik. 2016. Using news articles for real-time cross-lingual event detection and filtering. In *ECIR*.

Christopher D Manning, Prabhakar Raghavan, Hinrich Schütze, et al. 2008. *Introduction to information retrieval*, volume 1. Cambridge university press Cambridge.

Pavol Navrat, Lucia Jastrzembska, and Tomas Jelinek. 2009. Bee hive at work: Story tracking case study. In *WI-IAT'09. IEEE/WIC/ACM*, volume 3. IET.

Tadashi Nomoto. 2015. Mediameter: A global monitor for online news coverage. *ACL-IJCNLP 2015*, page 30.

Gevorg Poghosyan, M. Atif Qureshi, and Georgiana Ifrim. 2016. Topy: Real-time story tracking via social tags. In *ECMLPKDD*.

Bruno Pouliquen, Ralf Steinberger, and Olivier Deguernel. 2008. Story tracking: linking similar news over time and across languages. In *MMIES*.

Stephen E. Robertson, Steve Walker, Susan Jones, Micheline Hancock-Beaulieu, and Mike Gatford. 1994. Okapi at trec-3. In *TREC*.

Rodrygo LT Santos, Jie Peng, Craig Macdonald, and Iadh Ounis. 2010. Explicit search result diversification through sub-queries. In *ECIR*.

Bichen Shi, Georgiana Ifrim, and Neil Hurley. 2016. Learning-to-rank for real-time high-precision hashtag recommendation for streaming news. In *WWW*.

Suzan Verberne, Thymen Wabeke, and Rianne Kaptein. 2016. Boolean queries for news monitoring: Suggesting new query terms to expert users. In *ECIR*.

Piek Vossen, Tommaso Caselli, and Yiota Kontzopoulou. 2015. Storylines for structuring massive streams of news. *ACL-IJCNLP 2015*, page 40.

Mohammed Javeed Zaki. 2000. Scalable algorithms for association mining. *IEEE Transactions on Knowledge and Data Engineering*, 12(3):372–390.

# Nonparametric Bayesian Storyline Detection from Microtexts


**Vinodh Krishnan**
Georgia Institute of Technology
Atlanta, GA 30308
`krishnan.vinodh@gmail.com`

**Jacob Eisenstein**
Georgia Institute of Technology
Atlanta, GA 30308
`jacobe@gmail.com`



## Abstract

News events and social media are composed of evolving storylines, which capture public attention for a limited period of time. Identifying storylines requires integrating temporal and linguistic information, and prior work takes a largely heuristic approach. We present a novel online non-parametric Bayesian framework for storyline detection, using the distance-dependent Chinese Restaurant Process (dd-CRP). To ensure efficient linear-time inference, we employ a fixed-lag Gibbs sampling procedure, which is novel for the dd-CRP. We evaluate on the TREC Twitter Timeline Generation (TTG), obtaining encouraging results: despite using a weak baseline retrieval model, the dd-CRP story clustering method is competitive with the best entries in the 2014 TTG task.


## 1 Introduction

A long-standing goal for information retrieval and extraction is to identify and group textual references to ongoing events in the world (Allan, 2002). Success on this task would have applications in personalized news portals (Gabrilovich et al., 2004), intelligence analysis, disaster relief (Vieweg et al., 2010), and in understanding the properties of the news cycle (Leskovec et al., 2009). This task attains a new importance in the era of social media, where citizen journalists can document events as they unfold (Lotan et al., 2011), but where repetition and untrustworthy information can make the reader's task especially challenging (Becker et al., 2011; Marcus et al., 2011; Petrović et al., 2010).

A major technical challenge is in fusing information from two heterogeneous data sources: textual content and time. Two different documents about a single event might use very different vocabulary, particularly in sparse social media data such as microblogs; conversely, two different sporting events might be described in nearly identical language, with differences only in the numerical outcome. Temporal information is therefore critical: in the first case, to find the commonalities across disparate writing styles, and in the second case, to identify the differences. A further challenge is that unlike in standard document clustering tasks, the number of events in a data stream is typically unknown in advance. Finally, there is a high premium on scalability, since online text is produced at a high rate.

Due to these challenges, existing approaches for combining these modalities have been somewhat heuristic, relying on tunable parameters to control the tradeoff between textual and temporal similarity. In contrast, the Bayesian setting provides elegant formalisms for reasoning about latent structures (e.g., events) and their stochastically-generated realizations across text and time. In this paper, we describe one such model, based on the distance-dependent Chinese Restaurant Process (dd-CRP; Blei and Frazier, 2011). This model is distinguished by the neat separation that it draws between textual content, which is treated as a stochastic emission from an unknown Multinomial distribution, and time, which is modeled as a prior on graphs over documents, through an arbitrary *distance function*. However, straightforward implementations of the dd-CRP are insufficiently scalable, and so the model




*Proceedings of 2nd Workshop on Computing News Storylines*, pages 30–35,
Austin, TX, November 5, 2016. ©2016 Association for Computational Linguistics

has been relatively underutilized in the NLP literature (Titov and Klementiev, 2011; Kim and Oh, 2011; Sirts et al., 2014). We describe improvements to Bayesian inference that make the application of this model feasible, and present encouraging empirical results on the Tweet Timeline Generation task from TREC 2014 (Lin et al., 2014).

## 2   Model

The basic task that we address is to group short text documents into an unknown number of storylines, based on their textual content and their temporal signature. The textual content may be extremely sparse — the typical Tweet is on the order of ten words long — so leveraging temporal information is crucial. Moreover, the temporal signal is multiscale: in the 24-hour news cycle, some storylines last for less than an hour, while others, like the disappearance of the Malaysian Airlines 370 plane in 2014, continue for weeks or months. In some cases, the temporal distribution of references to a storyline will be unimodal and well-described by a parametric model (Marcus et al., 2011); in other cases, it may be irregular, with bursts of activity followed by periods of silence (He et al., 2007). Finally, it will be crucial to produce an implementation that scales to large corpora.

The distance-dependent Chinese Restaurant Process (dd-CRP) meets many of these criteria (Blei and Frazier, 2011). In this model, the key idea is that each instance (document) $i$ "follows" another instance $c_i$ (where it is possible that $c_i = i$), inducing a graph. We can compute a partitioning over instances by considering the connected components in the undirected version of the follower graph; these partitions correspond to "tables" in the conventional "Chinese Restaurant" analogy (Aldous, 1985), or to clusters. The advantage of this approach is that it is fundamentally non-parametric, and it introduces a clean separation between the textual data and the covariates: the text is generated by a distribution associated with the partition, while the covariates are associated with the following links, which are conditioned on a distance function.

The distribution over follower links for document $i$ has the following form,

$$\Pr(c_i = j) \propto \begin{cases} f(d_{i,j}), & i \neq j \\ \alpha, & i = j, \end{cases} \qquad (1)$$

where $d_{i,j}$ is the distance between units $i$ and $j$, and $\alpha > 0$ is a parameter of the model. Large values of $\alpha$ induce more self-links and therefore more fine-grained partitionings. Since we are concerned with temporal covariates, we define the distance function as follows:

$$f(d_{i,j}) = e^{\frac{-|t_i - t_j|}{a}}. \qquad (2)$$

Thus, the likelihood of document $i$ following document $j$ decreases exponentially as the time gap $|t_i - t_j|$ increases.

The text of each document $i$ is represented by a vector of word counts $w_i$. The likelihood distribution is multinomial, conditioned on a parameter $\theta$ associated with the partition to which document $i$ belongs. By placing a Dirichlet prior on $\theta$, we can analytically integrate it out. Writing $z^{(c)}$ for the cluster membership induced by the follower graph $c$, we have:

$$P(w \mid c; \eta) = \prod_k P(\{w_i : z_i^{(c)} = k\}; \eta) \qquad (3)$$

$$= \prod_k \int_\theta P(\{w_i : z_i^{(c)} = k\} \mid \theta) P(\theta; \eta) d\theta \qquad (4)$$

Given a multinomial likelihood $P(w \mid \theta)$ and a (symmetric) Dirichlet prior $P(\theta \mid \eta)$, this integral has a closed-form solution as the Dirichlet-Multinomial distribution (also known as the multivariate Polya distribution). The joint probability is therefore equal to the product of Equation 1 and Equation 4,

$$P(w, c) = \prod_i P(c_i; \alpha, a) \prod_k P(\{w_i : z_i^{(c)} = k\}; \eta). \qquad (5)$$

The model has three hyperparameters: $\alpha$, which controls the likelihood of self-linking, and therefore affects the number of clusters; $a$, which controls the time scale of the distance function, and therefore affects the importance of the temporal dimension to the resulting clusters; and $\eta$, which controls the precision of the Dirichlet prior, and therefore the importance of rare words in the textual likelihood function.

Estimation of these hyperparameters is described in § 3.2.

## 3 Inference

The key sampling equation for the dd-CRP is the posterior likelihood,

$$\Pr(c_i = j \mid \boldsymbol{c}_{-i}, \boldsymbol{w}) \propto \Pr(c_i = j) P(\boldsymbol{w} \mid \boldsymbol{c}).$$

The prior is defined in Equation 1. Let $\ell$ represent the likelihood under the partitioning induced when the link $c_i$ is cut. Now, the likelihood term has two cases: in the first case, $j$ is already in the same connected component as $i$ (even after cutting the link $c_i$), so no components are merged by setting $c_i = j$. In this case, the likelihood $P(\boldsymbol{w} \mid c_i = j)$ is exactly equal to $\ell$. In the second case, setting $c_i = j$ causes two clusters to be merged. This gives the likelihood,

$$P(\boldsymbol{w} \mid c_i = j, \boldsymbol{c}_{-i})$$

$$\propto \frac{P(\{\boldsymbol{w}_k : z_k^{(c)} = z_j^{(c)} \vee z_k^{(c)} = z_i^{(c)}\})}{P(\{\boldsymbol{w}_k : z_k^{(c)} = z_i^{(c)}\}) P(\{\boldsymbol{w}_k : z_k^{(c)} = z_j^{(c)}\})},$$

where the constant of proportionality is exactly equal to $\ell$. Each of the terms in the likelihood ratio is a Dirichlet Compound Multinomial likelihood. This likelihood function is itself a ratio of gamma functions; by eliminating constant terms and exploiting the identity $\Gamma(x + 1) = x\Gamma(x)$, we can reduce the number of Gamma function evaluations required to compute this ratio to the number of words which appear in *both* clusters $z_i^{(c)}$ and $z_j^{(c)}$. Words that occur in neither cluster can safely be ignored, and the gamma functions for words which occur in exactly one of the two clusters cancel in the numerator and denominator of the ratio. Note also that we only need compute the likelihood for $c_i$ with respect to each cluster, not for every possible follower link.

### 3.1 Online inference

While we make every effort to accelerate the computation of individual Gibbs samples, the complexity of the basic algorithm is superlinear in the number of instances. This is due to the fact that each sample requires computing the probability of instance $i$ joining every possible cluster, while the number of clusters itself grows with the number of instances

(this growth is logarithmic in the Chinese Restaurant Process). Scalability to the streaming setting therefore requires more aggressive optimizations.

To get back to linear time complexity, we employ a fixed-lag sampling procedure (Doucet et al., 2000). After receiving instance $i$, we perform Gibbs sampling only within the fixed window $[t_i - \tau, t_i]$, leaving $c_j$ fixed if $t_j < t_i - \tau$. This approximate sampling procedure implicitly changes the underlying model, because there is no possibility of linking $i$ to a later message $j$ if the time gap $t_j - t_i > \tau$.

Since we are only interested in obtaining a single storyline clustering — rather than a full Bayesian distribution over clusterings — we perform annealing for samples towards the end of the sampling window. Specifically, we set the temperature to $\gamma = 2.0$ and exponentiate the sampling likelihood by the inverse temperature (Geman and Geman, 1984). This has the effect of interpolating between probabilistically-correct Gibbs sampling and a hard coordinate-ascent procedure.

### 3.2 Hyperparameter estimation

The model has three parameters to estimate:

- $\alpha$, the concentration parameter of the dd-CRP
- $a$, the offset of the distance function
- $\eta$, the scale of the symmetric Dirichlet prior.

We interleave maximization-based updates to these parameters with sampling, in a procedure inspired by Monte Carlo Expectation Maximization (Wei and Tanner, 1990). Specifically, we compute gradients on the likelihood $P(\boldsymbol{c})$ with respect to $\alpha$ and $a$, and take gradient steps after every fixed number of samples. For the symmetric Dirichlet parameter $\eta$, we employ the heuristic from Minka (2012) by setting the parameter to $\eta = \frac{(K-1)/2}{\sum_k \log p_k}$, where $K$ is the number of words that appear exactly once, and $p_k$ is the probability of choosing the $k^{th}$ word from the vocabulary under the unigram distribution for the entire corpus.

## 4 TREC Evaluation

To test the efficacy of this approach, we evaluate on the Twitter Timeline Generation (TTG) task in the Microblog track of TREC 2014. It involves taking tweets based on a query $Q$ at time $T$ and returning a summary that captures relevant information. We perform the task on 55 queries with different timestamps and compare our results with 13 groups that submitted 50 runs for this task in 2014.

We consider the following systems:

**Baseline** We replace the distance-dependent prior with a standard Dirichlet prior. The number of clusters is heuristically set to 20. Annealed Gibbs sampling is employed for inference.

**Offline inference** The dd-CRP model with offline inference procedure (described in § 3).

**Online inference** The dd-CRP model with online inference procedure (described in § 3.1).

For the online inference implementation, we set the size of window and number of iterations to five days and 500 respectively. For the baseline, the parameter of the Dirichlet prior was set to a vector of 0.5 for each cluster. These values were chosen through 10-fold cross validation.

To measure the quality of the clusterings obtained by these models, we compare the average weighted and unweighted F-measures for 55 TREC topics, using the evaluation scripts from the TREC TTG task. Overall results are shown in Table 1. The ONLINE MODEL has the best weighted F1 score, outperforming the offline version of the same model, even though its inference procedure is an approximation to the OFFLINE MODEL. It may be that its approximate inference procedure discourages long-range linkages, thus placing a greater emphasis on the temporal dimension. Both models were trained over 500 iterations, and the ONLINE MODEL was 30% faster to train than the offline model.

Compared to the other 2014 TREC TTG systems, our dd-CRP models are competitive. Both models outperform all but one of the fourteen submissions on the unweighted $F_1$ metric, and would have placed fourth on the weighted $F_1^w$ metric. Note that the TREC evaluation scores both clustering quality and retrieval. We use only the baseline retrieval model, which achieved a mean average precision of 0.31. The competing systems shown in Table 1 all use retrieval models that are far superior: the retrieval model for top-ranked PKUICST team (line 4) achieved a mean average precision (MAP) of 0.59 (Lv et al., 2014), and the QCRI (Magdy et al.,

2014) and and hltcoe (Xu et al., 2014) teams (lines 5 and 6) used retrieval models with MAP scores of at least 0.5. Bayesian dd-CRP storyline clustering was competitive with these timeline generation systems despite employing a far worse retrieval model, so improving the retrieval model to achieve parity with these alternative systems seems the most straightforward path towards better overall performance.

## 5   Related work

Topic tracking and first-story detection are very well-studied tasks; space does not permit a complete analysis of the related work, but see (Allan, 2002) for a summary of "first generation" research. More recent non-Bayesian approaches have focused on string overlap (Suen et al., 2013), submodular optimization (Shahaf et al., 2012), and locality-sensitive hashing (Petrović et al., 2010). In Bayesian storyline analysis, the seminal models are Topics-Over-Time (Wang and McCallum, 2006), which associates a parametric distribution over time with each topic (Ihler et al., 2006), and the Dynamic Topic Model (Blei and Lafferty, 2006), which models topic evolution as a linear dynamical system (Nallapati et al., 2007). Later work by Diao et al. (2012) offers a model for identifying "bursty" topics, with inference requiring dynamic programming. All these approaches require the number of topics to be identified in advance. Kim and Oh (2011) apply a distance-dependent Chinese Restaurant *Franchise* for temporal topic modeling; they evaluate using predictive likelihood rather than comparing against ground truth, and do not consider online inference.

The Infinite Topic-Cluster model (Ahmed et al., 2011a) is non-parametric over the number of storylines, through the use of the recurrent Chinese Restaurant Process (rCRP). The model is substantially more complex than our approach. Unlike the dd-CRP, the rCRP is Markovian in nature, so that the topic distribution at each point in time is conditioned on the previous epoch (or, at best, the previous $K$ epochs, with complexity of inference increasing with $K$). This Markovian assumption creates probabilistic dependencies between the topic assignment for a given document and the documents that follow in subsequent epochs, necessitating an inference procedure that combines sequential

| Model | Rec. | Rec.$^w$ | Prec. | $F_1$ | $F_1^w$ |
|---|---|---|---|---|---|
| *Our clustering models* | | | | | |
| 1. BASELINE | 0.14 | 0.27 | 0.33 | 0.20 | 0.30 |
| 2. OFFLINE | 0.32 | 0.47 | 0.27 | 0.29 | 0.34 |
| 3. ONLINE | 0.34 | 0.55 | 0.26 | 0.29 | 0.35 |
| *Top systems from Trec-2014 TTG* | | | | | |
| 4. TTGPKUICST2 (Lv et al., 2014) | 0.37 | 0.58 | 0.46 | 0.35 | 0.46 |
| 5. EM50 (Magdy et al., 2014) | 0.29 | 0.48 | 0.42 | 0.25 | 0.38 |
| 6. hltcoeTTG1 (Xu et al., 2014) | 0.40 | 0.59 | 0.34 | 0.28 | 0.37 |

**Table 1:** Performance of Models in the TREC 2014 TTG Task. Weighted recall and $F_1$ are indicated as Rec.$^w$ and $F_1^w$.

Monte Carlo and Metropolis Hastings, and a custom data structure; this inference procedure was complex enough to warrant a companion paper (Ahmed et al., 2011b). The rCRP is also employed by Diao and Jiang (2013, 2014). In contrast, the dd-CRP makes no Markovian assumptions, and efficient inference is possible through relatively straightforward Gibbs sampling in a fixed window.

## 6 Conclusion

We present a simple non-parametric model for clustering short documents (such as tweets) into storylines, which are conceptually coherent and temporally focused. Future work may consider learning more flexible temporal distance functions, which could potentially represent temporal periodicity or parametric models of content popularity.

## Acknowledgments

We thank the reviewers for their helpful feedback. This research was supported by an award from the National Institutes for Health (R01GM112697-01), and by Google, through a Focused Research Award for Computational Journalism.

## References

Amr Ahmed, Qirong Ho, Jacob Eisenstein, Eric Xing, Alexander J. Smola, and Choon H. Teo. 2011a. Unified analysis of streaming news. In *WWW*, pages 267–276, Hyderabad, India.

Amr Ahmed, Qirong Ho, Choon H Teo, Jacob Eisenstein, Eric P Xing, and Alex J Smola. 2011b. Online inference for the infinite topic-cluster model: Storylines from streaming text. In *AISTATS*, pages 101–109, Fort Lauderdale, FL.

David J Aldous. 1985. *Exchangeability and related topics*. Springer.

James Allan. 2002. *Topic detection and tracking: event-based information organization*, volume 12. Springer Science & Business Media.

Hila Becker, Mor Naaman, and Luis Gravano. 2011. Beyond trending topics: Real-world event identification on twitter. In *Proceedings of the International Conference on Web and Social Media (ICWSM)*, pages 438–441.

David M Blei and Peter I Frazier. 2011. Distance dependent chinese restaurant processes. *The Journal of Machine Learning Research*, 12:2461–2488.

David M Blei and John D Lafferty. 2006. Dynamic topic models. In *Proceedings of the 23rd international conference on Machine learning*, pages 113–120. ACM.

Qiming Diao and Jing Jiang. 2013. A unified model for topics, events and users on twitter. In *Proceedings of Empirical Methods for Natural Language Processing (EMNLP)*.

Qiming Diao and Jing Jiang. 2014. Recurrent chinese restaurant process with a duration-based discount for event identification from twitter. In *The 18th Pacific-Asia Conference on Knowledge Discovery and Data Mining (SDM'14)*.

Qiming Diao, Jing Jiang, Feida Zhu, and Ee-Peng Lim. 2012. Finding bursty topics from microblogs. In *Proceedings of the Association for Computational Linguistics (ACL)*, pages 536–544, Jeju, Korea.

Arnaud Doucet, Simon Godsill, and Christophe Andrieu. 2000. On sequential monte carlo sampling methods for bayesian filtering. *Statistics and computing*, 10(3):197–208.

Evgeniy Gabrilovich, Susan Dumais, and Eric Horvitz. 2004. Newsjunkie: providing personalized newsfeeds via analysis of information novelty. In *Proceedings of the 13th international conference on World Wide Web*, pages 482–490. ACM.

Stuart Geman and Donald Geman. 1984. Stochastic relaxation, gibbs distributions, and the bayesian restoration of images. *IEEE Transactions on Pattern Analysis and Machine Intelligence*, pages 721–741.

Qi He, Kuiyu Chang, and Ee-Peng Lim. 2007. Analyzing feature trajectories for event detection. In *SIGIR*, pages 207–214. ACM.

Alexander Ihler, Jon Hutchins, and Padhraic Smyth. 2006. Adaptive event detection with time-varying poisson processes. In *KDD*, pages 207–216. ACM.

Dongwoo Kim and Alice Oh. 2011. Accounting for data dependencies within a hierarchical dirichlet process mixture model. In *cikm*, pages 873–878.

Jure Leskovec, Lars Backstrom, and Jon Kleinberg. 2009. Meme-tracking and the dynamics of the news cycle. In *Proceedings of Knowledge Discovery and Data Mining (KDD)*, pages 497–506.

Jimmy Lin, Miles Efron, Yulu Wang, and Garrick Sherman. 2014. Overview of the trec-2014 microblog track. In *Proceedings of the Twenty-Third Text REtrieval Conference*.

Gilad Lotan, Erhardt Graeff, Mike Ananny, Devin Gaffney, Ian Pearce, and danah boyd. 2011. The arab spring— the revolutions were tweeted: Information flows during the 2011 tunisian and egyptian revolutions. *International journal of communication*, 5:31.

Chao Lv, Feifan Fan, Runwei Qiang, Yue Fei, and Jianwu Yang. 2014. PKUICST at TREC 2014 Microblog Track: feature extraction for effective microblog search and adaptive clustering algorithms for TTG. Technical report, DTIC Document.

Walid Magdy, Wei Gao, Tarek Elganainy, and Zhongyu Wei. 2014. Qcri at trec 2014: applying the kiss principle for the ttg task in the microblog track. Technical report, DTIC Document.

Adam Marcus, Michael S Bernstein, Osama Badar, David R Karger, Samuel Madden, and Robert C Miller. 2011. Twitinfo: aggregating and visualizing microblogs for event exploration. In *chi*, pages 227–236. ACM.

Thomas Minka. 2012. Estimating a dirichlet distribution. `http://research.microsoft.com/en-us/um/people/minka/papers/dirichlet/minka-dirichlet.pdf`.

Ramesh M Nallapati, Susan Ditmore, John D Lafferty, and Kin Ung. 2007. Multiscale topic tomography. In *KDD*, pages 520–529. ACM.

Saša Petrović, Miles Osborne, and Victor Lavrenko. 2010. Streaming first story detection with application to twitter. In *Proceedings of the North American Chapter of the Association for Computational Linguistics (NAACL)*, pages 181–189, Los Angeles, CA.

Dafna Shahaf, Carlos Guestrin, and Eric Horvitz. 2012. Trains of thought: Generating information maps. In *Proceedings of the Conference on World-Wide Web (WWW)*, pages 899–908, Lyon, France. ACM.

Kairit Sirts, Jacob Eisenstein, Micha Elsner, and Sharon Goldwater. 2014. Pos induction with distributional and morphological information using a distance-dependent chinese restaurant process. In *Proceedings of the Association for Computational Linguistics (ACL)*, Baltimore, MD.

Caroline Suen, Sandy Huang, Chantat Eksombatchai, Rok Sosic, and Jure Leskovec. 2013. Nifty: a system for large scale information flow tracking and clustering. In *Proceedings of the Conference on World-Wide Web (WWW)*, pages 1237–1248.

Ivan Titov and Alexandre Klementiev. 2011. A bayesian model for unsupervised semantic parsing. In *Proceedings of the 49th Annual Meeting of the Association for Computational Linguistics: Human Language Technologies-Volume 1*, pages 1445–1455. Association for Computational Linguistics.

Sarah Vieweg, Amanda L. Hughes, Kate Starbird, and Leysia Palen. 2010. Microblogging during two natural hazards events: What twitter may contribute to situational awareness. In *Proceedings of the SIGCHI Conference on Human Factors in Computing Systems*, CHI '10, pages 1079–1088, New York, NY, USA. ACM.

Xuerui Wang and Andrew McCallum. 2006. Topics over time: a non-markov continuous-time model of topical trends. In *Proceedings of the 12th ACM SIGKDD international conference on Knowledge discovery and data mining*, pages 424–433. ACM.

Greg CG Wei and Martin A Tanner. 1990. A monte carlo implementation of the em algorithm and the poor man's data augmentation algorithms. *Journal of the American Statistical Association*, 85(411):699–704.

Tan Xu, Paul McNamee, and Douglas W Oard. 2014. Hltcoe at trec 2014: Microblog and clinical decision support.

# Automatic Identification of Narrative Diegesis and Point of View

**Joshua D. Eisenberg** and **Mark A. Finlayson**
11200 S.W. 8th Street, ECS Building, Miami, FL 33141
School of Computing and Information Sciences
Florida International University
{jeise003, markaf}@fiu.edu

## Abstract

The style of narrative news affects how it is interpreted and received by readers. Two key stylistic characteristics of narrative text are *point of view* and *diegesis*: respectively, whether the narrative recounts events personally or impersonally, and whether the narrator is involved in the events of the story. Although central to the interpretation and reception of news, and of narratives more generally, there has been no prior work on automatically identifying these two characteristics in text. We develop automatic classifiers for point of view and diegesis, and compare the performance of different feature sets for both. We built a gold-standard corpus where we double-annotated to substantial agreement ($\kappa > 0.59$) 270 English novels for point of view and diegesis. As might be expected, personal pronouns comprise the best features for point of view classification, achieving an average $F_1$ of 0.928. For diegesis, the best features were personal pronouns and the occurrences of first person pronouns in the argument of verbs, achieving an average $F_1$ of 0.898. We apply the classifier to nearly 40,000 news texts across five different corpora comprising multiple genres (including newswire, opinion, blog posts, and scientific press releases), and show that the point of view and diegesis correlates largely as expected with the nominal genre of the texts. We release the training data and the classifier for use by the community.

## 1 Introduction

Interpreting a text's veridicality, correctly identifying the implications of its events, and properly de-

limiting the scope of its references are all challenging and important problems that are critical to achieving complete automatic understanding of news stories and, indeed, text generally. There has been significant progress on some of these problems for certain sorts of texts, for example, recognizing implications on short, impersonal, factual text in the long-running Recognizing Textual Entailment challenge (RTE[1]). On the other hand, narrative text (including much news writing) presents additional complications, in that to accomplish the tasks above one must take into account the narrator's *point of view* (i.e., first person or third person), as well as the narrator's personal involvement in the story (a feature that narratologists call *diegesis*).

In news stories specifically writers are encouraged to use the third person point of view when they wish to emphasize their objectivity regarding the news they are reporting (Davison, 1983). In opinion pieces or blog posts, on the other hand, first person is more common and implies a more personal (and perhaps more subjective) view (Aufderheide, 1997). News writers are also often in the position of reporting on events which they themselves have not directly observed, and in these cases can use an uninvolved style (known as *hetereodiegetic* narration) to communicate their relative remove from the action. When writers observe or participate in events directly, however, or are reporting on their own lives (such as in blog posts), they can use an involved narrative style (i.e., *homodiegetic* narration) to emphasize their personal knowledge and subjective, perhaps biased, orientation.

---

[1] http://aclweb.org/aclwiki/index.php?title=RTE



*Proceedings of 2nd Workshop on Computing News Storylines*, pages 36–46,
Austin, TX, November 5, 2016. ©2016 Association for Computational Linguistics

Before we can integrate knowledge of point of view (POV) or diegesis into text understanding, we must be able to identify them, but there are no systems which enable automatic classification of these features. In this paper we develop reliable classifiers for both POV and diegesis, apply the classifiers to texts drawn from five different news genres, demonstrate the accuracy of the classifiers on these news texts, and show that the POV and diegesis correlates much as expected with the genre. We release the classifiers and the training data so the field may build on our work and integrate these features into other text processing systems.

Regarding the point of view of the narrator, narratologist Mieke Bal claimed "The different relationships of the narrative 'I' to the objects of narration are constant within each narrative text. This means that one can immediately, already on the first page, see which is the [point of view]." (Bal, 2009, p. 29) This assertion inspired the development of the classifiers presented here: we had annotators mark narrative POV and diegesis from the first 60 lines of each of 270 English novels, which is a generous simulation of "the first page". This observation allowed us to transform the collection of data for supervised machine learning from an unmanageable burden (i.e., having annotators read every novel from start to finish) into a tractable task (reading only the first page). We chose novels for training, instead of news texts themselves, because of the novels' greater diversity of language and style.

Once we developed reliable classifiers trained and tested with this annotated data, we applied the classifiers to 39,653 news-related texts across five news genres, including: the Reuter's corpus containing standard newswire reporting; a corpus of scientific press releases scraped from EurekAlerts; the CSC Islamist Extremist corpus containing ideological story telling, propaganda, and wartime press releases; a selection of opinion and editorial articles scraped from LexisNexis, the Spinn3r web blog corpus, and . We checked a sample of the results, confirming that the classifiers performed highly accurately over these genres. The classifiers allowed us to quickly assess the POV and diegesis of the texts and show how expectations of objectivity or involvement differ across genres.

The paper proceeds as follows. In §2 we define point of view and diegesis, and discuss their different attributes. In §3 we describe the annotation of the training and testing corpus, and then in §4 describe the development of the classifiers. In §5 we detail the results of applying the classifiers to the news texts. In §6 we outline related work, and in §7 we discuss how shortcomings of the work and how it might be improved. We summarize the contributions in §8. In short, this paper asks the qeustion: can point of view and deigesis be automatically classified? The experimental results in this paper show that it can be done.

## 2 Definitions

### 2.1 Point of View

The point of view (POV) of a narrative is whether the narrator describes events in a personal or impersonal manner. There are, in theory, three possible points of view, corresponding to grammatical person: first, second, and third person. First person point of view involves a narrator referring to themself, and implies a direct, personal observation of events. In a third person narrative, by contrast, the narrator is outside the storys course of action, looking in. The narrator tells the reader what happens to the characters of the story without ever referring to the narrator's own thoughts or feelings.

In theory second person POV is also possible, although exceedingly rare. In a second person narrative, the narrator tells the *reader* what he or she is feeling or doing, giving the impression that the narrator is speaking specifically to the reader themselves and perhaps even controlling their actions. This is a relatively rare point of view (in our training corpus of English novels it occurred only once), and because of this we exclude it from consideration.

Knowing the point of view (first or third person) is important for understanding the implied veridicality as well as the scope of references within the text. Consider the following example:

(1)    *John made everyone feel bad. He is a jerk.*

With regard to reference, if this is part of a first person narrative, the narrator is included in the scope of the pronoun *everyone*, implying that the narrator himself has been made to feel bad. In this case we might discount the objectivity of the second sentence if we know that the narrator himself feels bad on account of John. A third person narrator, by contrast, is excluded from the reference set, one can make no inference about his internal state and, thus, it does not affect our judgment of the implications of the accuracy or objectivity of later statements.

With regard to veridicality, if the narration is third person, statements of fact can be taken at face value with a higher default assumption of truthfulness. A first person narrator, in contrast, is experiencing the events not from an external, objective point of view but from a personal point of view, and so assessment of the truth or accuracy of their statements is subject to the same questions as a second-hand report.

## 2.2 Diegesis

Diegesis is whether the narrator is involved (homodiegetic) or not involved (heterodiegetic) in the story. In a homodiegetic narrative, the narrator is not just the narrator but a character as well, performing actions that drive the plot forward. In a heterodiegetic narrative, the narrator is observing the action but not influencing its course. As reflected in Table 1, third person narrators are almost exclusively heterodiegetic, but first person narrators can be either. Like point of view, diegesis provides information to the reader on how to discount statements of fact, and so to judge the veridicality of the text.

## 3 Corpus

To train and test our classifiers we chose a corpus of diverse texts and had it annotated for point of view and diegesis. We used the Corpus of English Novels (De Smet, 2008), which contains 292 English novels published between 1881 and 1922, and was assembled to represent approximately a generation of writers from turn-of-the-century English literature. Novels were included in the corpus if they were available freely from Project Gutenberg (Hart, 1971) when the corpus was assembled in 2007. There are twenty-five authors represented in the corpus, including, for example, Arthur Conan Doyle, Edith Wharton, and Robert Louis Stevenson. Genres represented span a wide range including drama, fantasy, adventure, historical fiction, and romance.

To simulate "the first page" of each novel, we manually trimmed each text file so that they started with the beginning of the first chapter. This was done by hand since automating this process was not a trivial task. Then, we automatically trimmed each file down to the first 60 lines, as defined by line breaks in the original files (which reflect the Gutenberg project's typesetting). These shortened texts were used by our annotators, and were the data on which the classifiers were trained and tested.

We wrote an annotation guide for point of view and diegesis, and trained two undergraduate students to perform the annotations. The first 20 books from the corpus were used to train the annotators, and the remaining 272 texts were annotated by both annotators. After annotation was complete we realized that two of the files erroneously contained text from the preface instead of the first chapter, so we removed them from our study. Minus the training and removed texts, we produced a gold-standard corpus of 270 novels annotated for point of view and diegesis.

### 3.1 Inter-annotator Agreement

We evaluated the inter-annotator agreement using Cohen's kappa coefficient ($\kappa$). For point of view $\kappa$ was 0.635, which is considered substantial (Landis and Koch, 1977). The $\kappa$ for diegesis is 0.592, almost substantial. Out of 270 markings, there were 36 and 33 conflicts between the annotators for POV and diegesis respectively. The first author resolved the conflicts in the POV and diegesis annotations by reading the text and determined the correct characteristic according to the annotation guide. We release this gold-standard corpus, including the annotation guide, for use by the community.[2]

### 3.2 Interaction of POV with Diegesis

Table 1 shows the distribution of the texts in the corpus across the various categories. Of the 270 texts in the corpus, 74 had first person narrators, only 1 had second person, and 195 were third person. For diegesis, 55 were homodiegetic and 215 were heterodiegetic. There was only one second person narrator; this type of narrator is atypical in narrative texts in general, and we excluded this text from training and testing.

---

[2]We have archived the code, annotated data, and annotation guide in the CSAIL Work Products section of the CSAIL Digital Archive, stored in the MIT DSpace online repository at https://dspace.mit.edu/handle/1721.1/29808.

|                    | First       | Second     | Third        |
| ------------------ | ----------- | ---------- | ------------ |
| **Homodiegetic**   | 54 (20%)    | 1 (0.4%)   | -            |
| **Heterodiegetic** | 20 (7.4%)   | -          | 195 (72.2%)  |

**Table 1:** Distribution of POV and Diegesis. Each non-zero entry lists the number of texts in the category as well as the percentage of the total corpus.

As we expected, there are no third person homdiegetic texts in the training corpus. Although in principle this is possible, it is narratively awkward, requires the narrator to be involved in the action of the story (homodiegetic), but report the events from a dispassionate, third-person point of view, never referring to themselves directly. Our data imply that this type of narrator is, at the very least, rare in turn of the century English literature. More generally, from our own incidental experience of narrative, we would expect this be quite rare across narrative in general.

## 4   Developing the Classifiers

We implemented the preprocessing (§4.1), SVM training, cross-validation testing (§4.2), and feature extraction for the classifiers (§4.3 and §4.4) in Java[3].

### 4.1   Preprocessing

The preprocessing was the same for both classifiers. The full text of the first 60 lines of the first chapter was loaded into a string, then all text within quotes was deleted using a regular expression. For both POV and diegesis it is important to focus on language that is uttered by the narrator, whereas quoted text represents words uttered by the characters of the narrative. The benefits of removing the quoted text is shown in Tables 3 and 4. After we removed the quoted text, we used the Stanford CoreNLP suite to tokenize and detect sentence boundaries (Manning et al., 2014). Finally, we removed all punctuation[4]). This produced an array of tokenized sentences, ready for feature extraction.

---

[3]We have archived a snapshot of the code, plus all the additional supplementary material, in the CSAIL Work Products section of the CSAIL Digital Archive, stored in the MIT DSpace online repository at https://dspace.mit.edu/handle/1721.1/29808.

[4]Specifically, the six characters [. ? ! , ; :].

### 4.2   Experimental Procedure

To determine the best sets of features for classification, we conducted two experiments, one each for POV and diegesis. In each case, texts were preprocessed as described above (§4.1), and various features were extracted as described below. Then we partitioned the corpus training and testing sets using ten-fold cross-validation. Precisely, this was done as follows: for POV, the texts annotated as first person were divided into ten sets containing nearly equal numbers of texts, and we did the same for the third person texts. Then the first set of both the first person and third person texts were designated as the test sets and the classifier was trained on the remaining nine sets from each class. This was repeated with each set (second, third, fourth, etc. . . . ), designating each set in order as the test set, with the remaining sets used for training. There are more third person narrators in the corpus; hence, each training fold has more examples of third person narrators than first person narrators. We performed cross-validation for diegesis in exactly the same manner.

We then trained an SVM classifier on the training fold using specific features as described below (Chang and Lin, 2011). To evaluate performance of the classifiers we report macro-averaged precision, recall, and $F_1$ measure. This is done by averaging, without any weighting, the precision, recall, and $F_1$ from each fold. We also report the average of $F_1$ for overall performance (weighted by number of texts).

### 4.3   Determining the Best POV Feature Set

The best set of features for point of view should be straightforward: narrators either refers to themselves (first person) or they don't (third person). Naturally, a first-person narrators will refer to themselves with first person pronouns, and so the presence of first person pronouns in non-quoted text should be a clear indicator of a first person point of view. Importantly, as soon as a narrator uses a first person pronoun they become a first person narrator, regardless of how long they were impersonally narrating. A list of the sets of first, second, and third person pronouns that we used as features can be found in Table 2.

We investigated eight different features sets for POV classification. The classifier with the best per-

| 1st | I, me, my, mine, myself, we, us, our, ours |
| 2nd | you, your, yours |
| 3rd | he, him, his, she, her hers, they, them, theirs |

**Table 2:** Pronouns used for classification.

formance uses counts of the first, second, and third person pronouns as the feature set. Six of the remaining experiments use different subsets of the pronouns: we test the performance of on each individual set of pronoun as well as each combination of two pronouns sets. Features sets that did not consider first person pronouns were unable to classify first person narrations, but, importantly, first person pronouns alone were not the best for classifying first person narratives. The classifier that considers all three types of pronouns has an $F_1$ almost six percentage points higher than the classifier that only considers first person pronouns.

Previously we discussed that it is important to remove quoted text before the features are extracted. To test this we ran an experiment where we did not remove quoted text in preprocessing, and then used all pronouns as in the best best performing classifier. This negatively impacted $F_1$ for first person narrators by 13 percentage points and the $F_1$ for third person narrators by about 3 percentage points. This shows that it is important to remove quoted text before extracting features for POV classification. The only feature sets that did worse than the feature set with quoted text removed were those feature sets that did not include first person pronouns.

### 4.4 Determining the Best Diegesis Feature Set

Pronouns are also a prominent feature of diegesis, but it is not as simple as counting which pronouns are used: diegesis captures the relationship of the narrator to the story. On the one hand, if the narrator never refers to themself (i.e., a third person narrator), then it is extremely unlikely that they are participating in the story they are telling, and so they are, by default, a heterodiegetic narrator. On the other hand, first person narrators may be either homo- or heterodiegetic. In this case one cannot merely count the number and type of pronouns that occur, but must pay attention to when first person pronouns, which represent the narrator, are used as arguments of verbs that represent events in the story. Event detection is a difficult task (Verhagen et al., 2007), so we focus on finding when first person pronouns are used as arguments of any verb. While in reality not all verbs represent events, a large fraction do, and as the performance of the classifier shows this feature correlates well with the category. To find the arguments of verbs, we use our in-house semantic role labeler (SRL) that is integrated into the Story Workbench (Finlayson, 2008; Finlayson, 2011).

We tested four different sets of features for diegesis classification. The simplest counts how many times each first person pronoun appears in an argument of a verb. Although this classifier is somewhat successful, it is somewhat weak identifying homodiegetic narrators.

The best performing diegesis classifier uses occurrences of the first, second, and third person pronouns in addition to the features from the simple diegesis classifier as features. We hypothesized that we could further improve the performance of this classifier by including a feature that counted the occurrences of second and third person pronouns as arguments of verbs that also have a first person pronoun as an argument (this is listed as the "co-occurrence" feature in Table 4). Our reasoning was that this feature would encode where the narrator and another character were connected by the same event, which is indicative of homodiegesis. Contrary to our expectations, however, this feature undermined homodiegetic classification: this classifier could not train an SVM model that could recognize homodiegetic narrators. This was the weakest of all of the diegesis classifiers.

Above we claimed that removal of quoted text is useful for diegesis classification. To show this, we took the feature set from our best diegesis classifier (with first person pronouns as arguments to a verb, and the occurrences of all pronouns), and took out the quoted text removal from the pipeline. This caused the $F_1$ measure to drop over 13 percentage points for homodiegetic and approximately 2 percentage points for heterodiegetic. These drops in performance indicate that the classifier performs better when quoted text is removed.

| Feature Set | Quoted Text Removed ↓ | First Person | | | Third Person | | | Avg. |
|---|---|---|---|---|---|---|---|---|
| | | Precision | Recall | $F_1$ | Precision | Recall | $F_1$ | $F_1$ |
| Majority class baseline | | 0 | 0 | 0 | 0.724 | 1 | 0.839 | 0.607 |
| 3rd person pronouns only | ✓ | 0 | 0 | 0 | 0.73 | 0.994 | 0.842 | 0.61 |
| 2nd person pronouns only | ✓ | 0 | 0 | 0 | 0.745 | 0.984 | 0.848 | 0.615 |
| 2nd & 3rd person pronouns | ✓ | 0 | 0 | 0 | 0.735 | 0.979 | 0.839 | 0.608 |
| All pronouns | | 0.911 | 0.671 | 0.743 | 0.893 | 0.963 | 0.924 | 0.874 |
| 1st person pronouns | ✓ | 0.969 | 0.7 | 0.793 | 0.903 | 0.989 | 0.943 | 0.902 |
| 1st & 3rd person pronouns | ✓ | 0.955 | 0.729 | 0.808 | 0.911 | 0.984 | 0.945 | 0.907 |
| 1st & 2nd person pronouns | ✓ | 0.94 | 0.757 | 0.814 | 0.921 | 0.974 | 0.944 | 0.908 |
| All pronouns | ✓ | 0.944 | 0.814 | **0.859** | 0.938 | 0.973 | **0.954** | **0.928** |

**Table 3:** Performance of point of view classification for different feature sets. The left hand column describes different sets of features used to train the SVM classifier. These features are extracted from the novels in the CEN. The columns to the right show the performance of each classifier when tested on CEN novels. Each data point is macro-averaged across the 10-folds of cross validation.

| Feature Set | Quoted Text Removed | | Homodiegetic | | | Heterodiegetic | | | Avg. |
|---|---|---|---|---|---|---|---|---|---|
| | All Pronouns ↳ | ↓ | Precision | Recall | $F_1$ | Precision | Recall | $F_1$ | $F_1$ |
| Majority class baseline | | | 0 | 0 | 0 | 0.796 | 1 | 0.886 | 0.706 |
| 1st pers. pronoun as verb arg. | | ✓ | 0.805 | 0.5 | 0.586 | 0.892 | 0.962 | 0.924 | 0.852 |
| 1st pers. as arg. + co-occurence | ✓ | ✓ | 0.847 | 0.480 | 0.589 | 0.889 | 0.976 | 0.93 | 0.858 |
| 1st pers. pronoun as verb arg. | | ✓ | 0.907 | 0.58 | 0.677 | 0.91 | 0.981 | 0.943 | 0.886 |
| 1st pers. pronoun as verb arg. | ✓ | ✓ | 0.931 | 0.62 | **0.721** | 0.917 | 0.981 | **0.947** | **0.898** |

**Table 4:** Performance of diegesis classification for different feature sets. The "co-occurence" feature is explained in the text. The left hand column describes different feature sets used to train the SVM classifier. These features are extracted from the novels in the CEN. The columns to the right show the performance of each classifier when tested on CEN novels. Each data point is macro-averaged across the 10-folds of cross validation.

## 5 Application of the Classifiers to News

To reveal the relationship of POV and diegesis to news story genres, we applied both classifiers a diverse set of news corpora. The classifiers for these experiments were trained on all 269 first and third person texts from the CEN,[5] using the best performing sets of features. We applied the classifiers to texts drawn from five corpora: the Reuters-21578 newswire corpus,[6] a corpus of scientific press releases scraped from EurekAlerts, a selection of opinion and editorial articles scraped from LexisNexis, the Spinn3r web blog corpus (Burton et al., 2009), and the CSC Islamist Extremist corpus containing ideological story telling, propaganda, and wartime press releases (Ceran et al., 2012). The stories from the Spinn3r web blog corpus were found by Gordon and Swanson (2009) and the CSC Islamist extremist stories were found by Ceran *et al.* (2012). These five corpora are used for testing the POV and diegesis classifiers; these corpora are not used for training the classifiers. For each experiment in this section, the best set of POV and diegesis features from S4.3 and §4.4, were used to train a classifier, these classifiers were trained on the first page of each novel from the CEN. For each corpora, after running the classifiers we randomly sampled texts and checked their classification to produce an estimate of the true accuracy of the classifiers. Sample sizes were determined by calculating the number of samples required to achieve a 99% confidence for a point estimate of proportion, using the proportion estimated by the classifier (Devore, 2011). In all cases the ratio of first person to third person texts (and homo- to hetero-diegetic texts) was chosen to be equal to the ratio in the classification.

---

[5]The number of texts was 269 because one text in the corpus of 270 texts was second person.

[6]http://www.daviddlewis.com/resources/testcollections/reuters21578/

## 5.1 Reuters-21578 Newswire

This corpus contains 19,043 texts, and all but one were marked by the classifiers as third person and heterodiegetic. We expected this, as journalists typically use the third person POV and heterodiegetic narration to communicate objectivity.

The erroneous classification of one text as first person was the result of a type of language we did not anticipate. The article in question uses direct speech to quote a letter written by Paul Volcker, Federal Reserve Board chair, to President Ronald Reagan. The majority of the article is the text of the letter, where Volcker repeatedly refers to himself, using the pronoun "I". The POV classifier interpreted this document at 1st person because the text of Volcker's letter was not removed in the quotation removal phase. The letter is quoted using direct speech, which our simple, regular-expression-based quotation detection system cannot recognize.

To estimate the true accuracy of the POV classifier over the Reuters corpus we randomly sampled and checked the POV of 200 texts (including the single first person text). All of the classifications were correct except the single first person text, resulting in an accuracy estimate of 99.5% over the newswire text for the POV classifier (1.3% margin of error at 99% confidence).

To estimate the true accuracy of the diegesis classifier over this corpus we randomly sampled and checked the diegesis of 200 texts (including the single homodiegetic text). Of the 199 heterodiegetic texts, all were correct, while the single homodiegetic text was incorrect, resulting in an accuracy estimate of 99% for the diegesis classifier over the newswire text (1.81% margin of error at 99% confidence).

## 5.2 EurekAlert Press Releases

This corpus contains 12,135 texts scraped from EurekAlert[7], dated between June 1st and December 31st, 2009. The distribution of this corpus is similar to the Reuters corpus, and over 99% of the texts were classified as third person and heterodiegetic narrations. Press offices write press releases to entice journalists to write newswire articles, and so it makes sense that they will attempt to mimic the desired narrative distance in the press release, seeking to present themselves as unbiased narrators.

To estimate the true accuracy of the POV classifier over the press releases we randomly sampled and checked the diegesis of 120 texts, including two first person and 118 third person. Of the two first person texts, one was correct, and of the 118 third person texts, 115 were correct, resulting in an accuracy estimate for the POV classifier of 97% over the press release text (4.03% margin of error at 99% confidence).

To estimate the true accuracy of the diegesis classifier over this corpus we randomly sampled and checked the diegesis of 120 texts, including 2 homodiegetic and 118 heterodiegetic. Of the two homodiegetic texts, neither were correct, and of the 118 heterodiegetic texts, 111 were correct, resulting in an accuracy estimate for the diegesis classifier of 94% over the press release text (5.6% margin of error at 99% confidence).

## 5.3 LexisNexis Opinions and Editorials

This corpus comprises 4,974 texts labeled opinion or editorial scraped from the LexisNexis website[8], dated between January 2012 and August 2016. Texts were included if they contained more than 100 words and appeared in one of a set of major world publications including, for example, the New York Times, the Washington Post, and the Wall Street Journal. About one-quarter of these texts are first person, and more than half of the first person narrators were homodiegetic. We expected this increased abundance of first person and homodiegetic texts, as the purpose of these types of articles is often to express individual opinions or the writer's personal experience of events.

To estimate the true accuracy of the POV classifier over the LexisNexis articles, we randomly sampled and checked the POV of 200 texts, 50 from those classified as first person and 150 from those classified as third person. Of the 50 texts classified as first person all were confirmed correct, while of the 150 texts classified as third person only 90 were confirmed correct. This suggests that our classifier is not properly identifying all of the first person narrators in the LexisNexis corpus, and results in a accuracy estimate of 70% for the POV classifier over

---

[7]http://www.eurekalert.org/

[8]http://www.lexisnexis.com/hottopics/lnacademic/

the LexisNexis texts (2.7% margin of error at 99% confidence).

To estimate the true accuracy of the diegesis classifier over this corpus we randomly sampled and checked the diegesis of 200 texts, including 24 homodiegetic and 126 heterodiegetic texts. Of the 24 homodiegetic texts, all were correct, and of the 126 heterodiegetic texts, 51 were correct, allowing us to estimate that the diegesis classifier has an accuracy of 40% over the press release text (11% margin of error at 99% confidence).

### 5.4  Spinn3r Web Blogs

This corpus comprises 201 stories extracted by Gordon and Swanson (2009) from the Spinn3r 2009 Web Blog corpus (Burton et al., 2009). These texts come from web blogs, where people often tell personal stories from their perspective, or use the blog as a public journal of their daily life. In contrast with newswire text, there is no expectation that a blog will report the truth in an unbiased manner. The distribution of the POV on this corpus reflects this tendency, with 66% of the texts being first person.

The diegesis distribution for the web blog stories was not unexpected: slightly more than half of the blog stories with first person narrators are homodiegetic. These are the most *personal* stories of the web blog story corpus, in which the narrator is involved in the story's action.

To estimate the true accuracy of the POV classifier on the Spinn3r corpus, we randomly sampled 20 texts, 13 from those classified as first person and 7 classified as third person. Of the 13 first person texts 9 were confirmed correct, while of the 7 third person texts only 3 were confirmed correct. Overall, our classifier has trouble classifying the web blog texts. This might be due to syntactic irregularities of blog posts, which vary in their degree of adherence to proper English grammar. With respect to third person narrators we estimate that the POV classifier has an accuracy of 42% over the web blog text (34% margin of error at 99% confidence).

To estimate the true accuracy of the diegesis classifier over this corpus we randomly sampled and checked the diegesis of 20 texts, including six homodiegetic and 14 heterodiegetic texts. Of the six homodiegetic texts, all were correct, and of the 14 heterodiegetic texts, three were correct. With re-

spect to the heterodiegetic narrators we estimate that the diegesis classifier has an accuracy of 21% over the press release text (27% margin of error at 99% confidence).

### 5.5  Islamic Extremist Texts

The CSC Islamist Extremist corpus contained 3,300 story texts, as identified by Corman *et al.* (2012). These texts were originally posted on Islamist Extremist websites or forums. Our POV classifier found that 99.7% of the extremist stories were written in the third person. For the most part, the extremist stories were second hand accounts of events, often to share news about the outcome of battles or recount the deeds of Jihadists.

To estimate the true accuracy of the POV classifier on this corpus, we randomly sampled 150 texts, 2 from those classified as first person, and 148 classified as third person. Both of the texts classified as first person were verified to be first person narrators. Of the 148 texts classified as third person, 139 were verified correct. With respect to third person narrators, we can estimate the classifier has an accuracy of 93.9% over the extremist texts (4.92% margin of error at 99% confidence).

To estimate the true accuracy of the diegesis classifier over this corpus we randomly sampled and checked the diegesis of 150 texts, including 2 homodiegetic and 148 heterodiegetic texts. Of the 2 homodiegetic texts, 1 was correct, and of the 148 heterodiegetic texts, 137. With respect to heterodiegtic narrators, we can estimate the classifier has an accuracy of 92% over the press release text (5.6% margin of error at 99% confidence).

## 6  Related Work

As far as we know this is the first study on the automatic classification of point of view and diegesis at the level of the text. In his book "Computational Modeling of Narrative", Mani framed the problem of computational classification of narrative characteristics, including point of view and diegesis, defining with reference to narratology (Mani, 2012). He gives a framework for representing features and characteristics of narrative in his markup language *NarrativeML*. However, he does not actually implement a classifier for these characteristics.

| Corpus | # Texts | 1st Person | 3rd Person | Homo. | Heterodiegetic | Accuracy Estm. |
|---|---|---|---|---|---|---|
| **Reuters-21578** | 19,043 | 1 ($<$1%) | 19,042 ($\sim$100%) | 1 ($<$1%) | 19042 ($\sim$100%) | 99% / 99% |
| **EurekAlert** | 12,135 | 31 ($<$1%) | 12,104 ($\sim$100%) | 5 ($<$1%) | 12,129 ($\sim$100%) | 97% / 94% |
| **CSC Extremist** | 3,300 | 42 (1%) | 3,258 (99%) | 15 ($<$1%) | 3,285 ($\sim$100%) | 94% / 92% |
| **Lexis Nexis** | 4,974 | 1,290 (26%) | 3,684 (74%) | 818 (16%) | 4,156 (84%) | 70% / 40% |
| **Spinn3r** | 201 | 133 (66%) | 68 (34%) | 67 (33%) | 134 (67%) | 42% / 21% |

**Table 5:** POV and Diegesis classifications of texts across corpora. Total number of texts was 39,653. The columns labeled "1st Person", "3rd Person", "Homo.", and "Heterodigetic" indicate the number of texts placed in each class by the classifiers trained on the CEN corpus. Percentages in parentheses indicate the fraction of that corpus falling into the specified category. The last column reports the measured accuracy of the classifiers as determined by randomly sampling and checking the results: the first percentage refers to the POV classifier and the second percentage to the diegesis classifier.

Wiebe proposed an algorithm for classifying psychological point of view in third person fictional narratives (Wiebe, 1994). The algorithm is a complex rule-based classifier which tracks broadening and narrowing of POV, and reasons whether each sentence is objective or subjective. She discusses a study where people used the algorithm to classify sentences, but the accuracy of people in that task was not given. Thus, while intriguing, it is not clear how well this algorithm performs since its correctness was not verified with a human annotated corpus.

In more recent work, Sagae *et al.* employed a data-driven approach for classifying spans of objective and subjective narrations (Sagae et al., 2013). Their experiments were performed on a corpus of 40 web blog posts from the Spinn3r 2009 web blog corpus (Burton et al., 2009). Their features included lexical, part of speech, and word/part of speech tag n-grams. The granularity of their classifier is fine grained, in that the system tags spans of text within a document, as opposed to our classifiers which classify the whole document.

## 7  Discussion

Our best classifier for POV uses the occurrence of all pronouns as features, with an $F_1$ of 0.857 for first person POV, and 0.954 for third person POV. The weighted average over the two classes is a 0.928 $F_1$. Table 3 contains the results for the POV classification experiments. This is a great start for the automatic classification of POV, and comes close to human performance. It is reasonable and expected from narratological discussion that the best set of features is the number of first, second, and third person pronouns in non-quoted text.

The best diegesis classifier in our study, the one that counts the first person pronouns as verb arguments as well as the occurrence of each pronoun, has an $F_1$ of 0.721 for homodiegetic, and 0.947 for heterodiegetic. The weighted average over the two classes is a 0.898 $F_1$. Table 4 contains the results for the diegesis classification experiments. This is a good first start for diegesis classification, but the performance for homodiegetic narrators falls short. The features for this classifier are also reasonable: first person pronouns in verb arguments shows that the narrator is either causing action to happen or being affected by actions, and so should naturally correlate with homodiegesis. The inclusion of all pronouns as a feature for diegesis also makes sense, as point of view and diegesis are closely correlated. As noted previously, third person narrators cannot refer to themselves, so they cannot be related to the story.

The best performing POV and diegesis classifiers performed signifcantly than their respective baseline classifiers. In Table 3, the majority class baseline classifier has 0.607 $F_1$, while the best POV classifier has 0.928 $F_1$. Table 4 shows that the majority baseline classifier for diegesis has 0.706 $F_1$, while the best diegesis classifier has 0.898 $F_1$.

Diegesis classification might be improved by restricting pronoun argument detection only to those verbs that actually indicate events in the story. This focuses the classifier on places where the narrator is involved in driving the story forward, which is more closely aligned with the definition of diegesis. To do this, we would need to incorporate an automatic event detector (Verhagen et al., 2007, e.g.). On the other hand, event detection currently is not especially accurate, and incorporating such a feature may very well depress our classification performance.

Another approach of interest would be to adapt our classifiers to detect if a narrative characteristic changes over the course of a text. Our study focused on short spans of traditional, formal, edited novels where the point of view and diegesis remained constant. In longer texts it is possible that these characteristics could change, for example, in a stream of text comprised of multiple narratives, or in a text which explicitly is trying to defy convention (e.g., in highly literary texts such as James Joyce's *Ulysses*).

Finally, our classifier assumed that the classified texts were all approximately the same length (i.e., the first page, or approximately 60 lines). A modification that would be important to explore is using densities or ratios for the occurrences of the pronouns, instead of raw counts, for classifying texts that are less than 60 lines long.

## 8  Contributions

In this paper, we described and made significant progress against the problem of automatic classification of narrative point of view and diegesis. We demonstrated a high performing classifier for point of view with 0.928 $F_1$, and a good classifier for diegesis with 0.898 $F_1$. To evaluate our classifiers we created a doubly annotated corpus with gold-standard annotations for point of view and diegesis–based on the first 60 lines–of 270 English novels. We applied these classifiers to almost 40,000 news story texts drawn from five different corpora, and show that the classifiers remain highly accurate and that the proportions of POV and diegesis they identify correlates in an expected way with the genre of the news texts. We provide the annotation guide, annotated corpus, and the software as resources for the community.

## Acknowledgments

This work was partially supported by National Institutes of Health (NIH) grant number 5R01GM105033-02. Thanks to Fernando Serrano and Victor Alvarez for their work annotating the Corpus of English Novels. We also thank Professor Steve Corman for providing access to his corpus of Islamic Extremist Texts.

## References

[Aufderheide1997] Patricia Aufderheide. 1997. Public intimacy: The development of first-person documentary. *Afterimage: The Journal of Media Arts and Cultural Criticism*, 25(1):16–18.

[Bal2009] Mieke Bal. 2009. *Narratology: Introduction to the Theory of Narrative*. University of Toronto Press, Toronto.

[Burton et al.2009] Kevin Burton, Akshay Java, and Ian Soboroff. 2009. The ICWSM 2009 Spinn3r dataset. In *Proceedings of the 3rd Annual Conference on Weblogs and Social Media (ICWSM 2009)*, San Jose, CA.

[Ceran et al.2012] Betul Ceran, Ravi Karad, Steven Corman, and Hasan Davulcu. 2012. A hybrid model and memory based story classifier. In *Proceedings of the 3rd International Workshop on Computational Models of Narrative (CMN'12)*, pages 60–64, Istanbul, Turkey.

[Chang and Lin2011] Chih-Chung Chang and Chih-Jen Lin. 2011. LIBSVM: A library for support vector machines. *ACM Transactions on Intelligent Systems and Technology (TIST)*, 2(3):1–27.

[Davison1983] W. Phillips Davison. 1983. The third-person effect in communication. *Public Opinion Quarterly*, 47(1):1–15.

[De Smet2008] Hendrik De Smet. 2008. Corpus of english novels. https://perswww.kuleuven.be/ u0044428/cen.htm.

[Devore2011] Jay L. Devore. 2011. *Probability and Statistics for Engineering and the Sciences*. Cengage Learning, Boston, MA, 8th edition.

[Finlayson2008] Mark A. Finlayson. 2008. Collecting semantics in the wild: The story workbench. In *Proceedings of the AAAI Fall Symposium on Naturally Inspired Artificial Intelligence (NIAI)*, pages 46–53, Arlington, VA.

[Finlayson2011] Mark A. Finlayson. 2011. The Story Workbench: An extensible semi-automatic text annotation tool. In *Proceedings of the 4th Workshop on Intelligent Narrative Technologies (INT4)*, pages 21–24, Stanford, CA.

[Gordon and Swanson2009] Andrew Gordon and Reid Swanson. 2009. Identifying personal stories in millions of weblog entries. In *Proceedings of the 3rd International Conference on Weblogs and Social Media (ICWSM 2009)*, Data Challenge Workshop, San Jose, CA.

[Hart1971] Michael Hart. 1971. Project Gutenberg. https://www.gutenberg.org/.

[Landis and Koch1977] Richard Landis and Gary Koch. 1977. The measurement of observer agreement for categorical data. *Biometrics*, 33(1):159–174.

[Mani2012] Inderjeet Mani. 2012. *Computational Modeling of Narrative*. Morgan & Claypool Publishers, Williston, VT.

[Manning et al.2014] Christopher D Manning, Mihai Surdeanu, John Bauer, Jenny Rose Finkel, Steven Bethard, and David McClosky. 2014. The Stanford CoreNLP natural language processing toolkit. In *Proceedings of the 52nd Annual Meeting of the Association for Computational Linguistics, System Demonstrations*, pages 55–60, Baltimore, MD.

[Sagae et al.2013] Kenji Sagae, Andrew Gordon, Morteza Dehghani, Mike Metke, Jackie Kim, Sarah Gimbel, Christine Tipper, Jonas Kaplan, and Mary Helen Immordino-Yang. 2013. A data-driven approach for classification of subjectivity in personal narratives. In *Proceedings of the 5th International Workshop on Computational Models of Narrative (CMN'13)*, pages 198–213, Hamburg, Germany.

[Verhagen et al.2007] Marc Verhagen, Robert Gaizauskas, Frank Schilder, Mark Hepple, Graham Katz, and James Pustejovsky. 2007. SemEval-2007 task 15: TempEval temporal relation identification. In *Proceedings of the 4th International Workshop on Semantic Evaluations (SemEval-2007)*, pages 75–80, Prague, Czech Republic.

[Wiebe1994] Janyce M Wiebe. 1994. Tracking point of view in narrative. *Computational Linguistics*, 20(2):233–287.

# Richer Event Description: Integrating event coreference with temporal, causal and bridging annotation


**Tim O'Gorman** and **Kristin Wright-Bettner** and **Martha Palmer**
Department of Linguistics
University of Colorado Boulder
Boulder CO 80309
`ogormant,kristin.wrightbettner,mpalmer@colorado.edu`



## Abstract

There have been a wide range of recent annotated corpora concerning events, either regarding event coreference, the temporal order of events, hierarchical "subevent" structure of events, or causal relationships between events. However, although some believe that these different phenomena will display rich interactions, relatively few corpora annotate all of those layers of annotation in a unified fashion. This paper describes the annotation methodology for the Richer Event Descriptions corpus, which annotates entities, events, times, their coreference and partial coreference relations, and the temporal, causal and subevent relationships between the events. It suggests that such rich annotations of within-document event phenomena can be built with high quality through a multi-stage annotation pipeline, and that the resultant corpus could be useful for systems hoping to transition from the detection of isolated mentions of events toward a richer understanding of events grounded in the temporal, causal, referential and bridging relations that define them.


## 1 Introduction

Many corpora have been released in the last decade and a half regarding the temporal order of events, the hierarchical "subevent" structure of events, causal relationships between events, or reference between events. However, the lack of large corpora annotated with all of those layers may hinder attempts to train systems that learn to jointly predict different phenomena. Furthermore, the low rates of interannotator agreement within event annotation are an ongoing issue for training and evaluating systems dealing with these phenomena.

The Richer Event Description (RED) corpus presents 95 documents (totaling 54287 tokens) sampled both from news data and casual discussion forum interactions, which contain 8731 events, 1127 temporal expressions (TIMEX3s, section time, and document time labels), and 10320 entity markables. It contains 2390 identity chains, 1863 bridging relations, and 4969 event-event relations encompassing temporal, causal and subevent relations (as well as aspectual ALINK relations and reporting relations), as well as 8731 DOCTIMEREL temporal annotations linking these events to the document time.

The fundamental contribution of the corpus is one in which a wide range of event-event and event coreference relations are annotated in a consistent and integrated manner. By capturing coreference, bridging, temporal, causal and subevent relations in the same annotation, the annotations may provide a more integrated sense of how the events in a particular document relate to each other, and encourage the development of systems that learn rich interactions between systems. Rich interactions between events in a text, moreover, may be useful for a wide range of goals; Liao and Grishman (2010) found that looking at related events within a document could aid ACE-style event detection, and Vossen et al. (2015) discussed the value of combining timelines with bridging and causal relations in the construction of storylines.

This paper covers the details of RED annotation, and illustrates a number of annotation methods used to overcome the challenges of annotating such a rich




*Proceedings of 2nd Workshop on Computing News Storylines*, pages 47–56,
Austin, TX, November 5, 2016. ©2016 Association for Computational Linguistics

inventory. We suggest that the advantages of annotating many different event-event phenomena at once can outweigh those challenges. Our corpus and guidelines will be made publicly available.

## 2   Related Work

Large-scale corpora for event detection and coreference exist in a number of forms. The original MUC tasks dealt with events and scenarios that fit within a particular ontology, and such ontology-driven event annotations have been extended through the ACE and ERE corpora and through the TAC-KBP evaluations (Humphreys et al. 1997, Bagga and Baldwin 1999, Song et al 2015). Unrestricted event coreference annotations were later developed in OntoNotes (Weischedel et al., 2011) – which annotated event coreference but did not explicitly differentiate events and entities – and in cross-document event corpora such as Lee et al. (2012), Cybulska and Vossen (2014), Minard et al (2016) and Hong et al. (2016).

Corpora for event-event and event-time relations have also been developed, both for temporal information in the TimeML tradition (Pustejovsky et al., 2003; Styler IV et al., 2014; Minard et al., 2016), and causal structure (Bethard, 2007; Mostafazadeh et al., 2016; Mirza et al., 2014; Hong et al., 2016; Dunietz et al., 2015). Subevent relations corpora have also been annotated (Glava and najder, 2014; Hong et al., 2016). In addition to those resources, there are many corpora which do not focus on annotating events directly, but which do annotate causal, temporal, event-structural or coreference relations within limited scopes, such as within the same clause or across adjacent sentences (Banarescu et al., 2013; Carlson et al., 2003; Prasad et al., 2008; Riaz and Girju, 2013; Fillmore and Baker, 2000; Palmer et al., 2005).

However, despite the profusion of corpora, only a few of the above resources attempt to provide an integrated annotation of many different event-event relations. Minard et al. (2016) annotated event and entity coreference and temporal relations (as well as semantic roles and cross-document coreference), but omitted both subevent structure and causal relations. Glavas and Snajder (2014) annotated event coreference and subevent relations, but did not capture tem-

poral or causal structure. Hong et al, (2016) annotated a wide inventory of event-event relations, but covered only events within the ERE ontology.

## 3   Discussion of Annotation

The process of RED annotation is divided into two passes, in order to maximize the quality of event annotations. In the first pass, annotators identify three types of markables: events, temporal expressions, and entities (participants such as people, organizations, objects, and locations). Specific properties of each event are also annotated in this pass, capturing information such as the relation to the document creation time or the modality of the event. Guidelines for these features largely following the Thyme-TimeML specifications (Styler IV et al., 2014), a modification of the ISO-TimeML (Pustejovsky et al., 2003) guidelines designed for clinical text. During that first pass, the entity markables are also annotated with coreference relations and bridging relations.

A second pass occurs only after that first pass is adjudicated, allowing all event-event relations to be labeled over adjudicated events and times. This reduces the propagation of errors from missed events or incorrect events, as the event-event relations and coreference are all annotated between high-quality adjudicated events. It also allows guidelines to be written assuming consistent treatment of event modality, allowing adjudicated modality features to be used when making coreference decisions.

### 3.1   First pass details and agreement

In many prior annotations such as OntoNotes (Weischedel et al., 2011), markables are only labeled if they participate in coreference chains. In RED annotation, events and entities are annotated regardless of whether they participate in a coreference chain. All occurrences and timeline-relevant states are annotated as events, and entities are annotated according to whether or not they represent an actual discourse referent in the discourse. Such an annotation could easily be adapted to OntoNotes-style annotation (by stripping out the singletons), but adds information that could be very useful for detection of the anaphoricity of mentions, a factor considered to be very useful in coreference resolution

(Harabagiu et al., 2001, Ng and Cardie 2002).

In RED annotation, these entities and events are also labeled using a minimal-span approach in which only the headwords are labeled. This annotation style may reduce the "span match" errors observed by (Kummerfeld and Klein, 2013) in recent systems, and some researchers working on coreference have observed the utility of focusing upon headwords, with (Peng et al., 2015) claiming that "identifying and co-referring mention heads is not only sufficient but is more robust than working with complete mentions" (Peng et al. 2015:1).

Richer Event Description also annotates events and entities with a representation of the polarity and modality of the events and entities in context, making a four-way distinction between AC-TUAL, GENERIC, HEDGED/UNCERTAIN, OR HY-POTHETICAL, and temporal expressions are distinguished into DATE, TIME, DURATION, QUANTI-FIER, PREPOSTEXP and SET, following the Thyme-TimeML annotation of clinical temporal expressions (Styler IV et al., 2014). Figure 1 shows both the accuracy of annotations on these phenomena, and the best performance of systems on a the Tempeval-2016 task, which was on the similarly annotated Thyme data. Modality guidelines were also added to allow annotation of entity modality, primarily to capture reference to generic entities.

A number of additional characteristics of events are annotated (such as intermittence (CONTEXTUAL ASPECT) and whether the event was explicit or implied), but the important additional feature is that of the DocTimeRel, or relationship to document time. Following the methodology of (Pustejovsky and Stubbs, 2011; Styler IV et al., 2014), annotators assume four implicit narrative containers within each document – BEFORE, OVERLAP, BE-FORE/OVERLAP or AFTER document time – and each event is labeled with the best such container. This obviates the necessity of labeling many of the more obvious temporal relations (such as knowing that events in the past happen before events in the future). As can be seen in Table 1, agreement of annotators with the adjudicated gold is very high for such DocTimeRel annotations, and system performance in the clinical domain for this kind of annotation is promising.

Coreference in the first pass is done between

| Markable | ITA | gold | TempEval2016 |
|---|---|---|---|
| Entity | 85.9 | 92.8 | |
| Event | 86.1 | 93.0 | 90.3 |
| Timex3 | 70.8 | 84.9 | 79.5 |
| **Features** | **ITA** | | |
| Timex3 class | 91.9 | 96.5 | 77.2 |
| Entity Modality | 92.3 | 96.5 | 85.1 |
| Event Polarity | 95.2 | 98.3 | 88.7 |
| Event Modality | 72.9 | 91.5 | 85.5 |
| Event DocTimeRel | 84.4 | 92.0 | 75.6 |

**Table 1:** Agreement F1 for Eventy, Event and TIMEX3 detection. Scores for features only measured when annotators agree that an event exists. Highest reported scores on Tempeval-2016 (a corpus annotated with similar event guidelines) are reported to give an approximation of system performance

all entities in the document, alongside annotation of apposition relations and three bridging relations. The bridging relations are important for capturing a range of anaphora phenomena that are not strict identity relationships (Clark, 1975; Poesio et al., 1997). SET/MEMBER was a label used both for set-subset and set-member relationships, PART/WHOLE captured relationships between entities that physically composed a larger whole, and a general BRIDGING relation was used for any class of bridging that did not fit into other categories, such as events of differing modality, allegations of identity (such as links between "the murderer" and a particular suspect).

The fact that this annotation explicitly labels modality and polarity features can have important consequences for coreference and bridging annotation. Even annotations which do not annotate genericity, such as OntoNotes coreference (Weischedel et al., 2011), have very specific rules about how they are annotated (in the case of OntoNotes, generics noun phrases are only linked to pronouns referring to them, or in specific headline constructions). This means that annotator behavior is dependent upon a separate decision (whether or not a markable is generic) that is never explicitly annotated. RED explicitly annotates modality, and constrains IDEN-TITY relations to only apply to be between elements with the same modality and polarity, and providing bridging relations to capture relations that do not pass this strict definition of identity. We evaluate entity coreference scores using the reference implementation of a variety of scoring metrics that was provided in (Pradhan et al., 2014), which are shown in Table 2. All agreement numbers are scored on a 55-document subset of the corpus sampled from discussion fora and newswire documents.

|            | muc   | bcub | ceafe | conll f1 |
|------------|-------|------|-------|----------|
| entity IAA | 75.3  | 68.5 | 67.6  | 70.4     |
| vs gold    | 80.06 | 85.0 | 79.5  | 81.8     |

Table 2: Agreement scores between annotators and agreement with gold, for Entity coreference

Table 3 shows the scores of entity-entity and event-event bridging relations.

| Entity     | ITA  | gold |
|------------|------|------|
| set/member | 21.5 | 46.5 |
| whole/part | 25.8 | 56.3 |
| bridging   | 7.1  | 25.6 |
| apposition | 51.2 | 67.6 |

Table 3: Agreement F1 scores on other entity coreference relations (Apposition, Set/Subset, Part/Whole and Bridging), both between annotators and when compared to adjudicated gold

We can also note the subset of this corpus used for agreement calculation was also annotated within the rich ERE paradigm (Song et al., 2015), which allows an inter-schema comparison of the overlap between a defined ontology of "relevant events" and the annotations presented here. 86.3% of all ERE Event mentions have strictly the same span as an Event annotated in RED, and that number grows to 89.5% when accommodating partial span matches. The missing 10.5% is largely due to markables which an annotation such as RED views as merely "entities" – rather than events – in RED annotations, as in the examples. This highlights the level to which corpora disagree on how to handle events that are entailed by entity mentions:

(1) These **nominees** have dedicated their careers to serving the public good, (ERE Personnel.nominate event)

(2) MILITANT SAYS HE IS BEHIND **FATAL** NIGER ATTACK (ERE Life.Die event)

The reverse is quite different, with only 25% of RED events having correlates in ERE, which are largely simply events that do not fit into the ontology used in (Song et al., 2015).

## 3.2 Event Coreference and Event Bridging

After the adjudication of event and entity markables, event coreference is done alongside the annotation of other event-event relations and event bridging relations. Annotating upon events after a markable adjudication pass is intended to increase consistency in how events are annotated. The annotation of event coreference alongside bridging, temporal, causal and subevent relations adds a different kind of consistency; because annotators cannot relate two event mentions in multiple ways, boundaries differentiating phenomena such as subevent and coreference phenomena are strictly defined, and guidelines are necessarily structured to make those boundaries clear-cut.

Table 4 shows coreference and bridging performance of the event annotations done in this second pass of annotation.

|            | muc    | bcub    | ceafe | conll f1 |
|------------|--------|---------|-------|----------|
| event IAA  | 68.2   | 65.1    | 63.2  | 65.5     |
| vs gold    | 84.5   | 82.8    | 82.3  | 83.2     |
| **Event**  | F1 IAA | vs gold |       |          |
| Set/subset | 25.1   | 64.6    |       |          |
| bridging   | 5.8    | 51.9    |       |          |

Table 4: Agreement scores between annotators and agreement with gold for event coreference

## 3.3 Temporal and Subevent Annotation

This annotation followed recent work in the TimeML tradition (Pustejovsky and Stubbs, 2011; Styler IV et al., 2014) in focusing upon informative temporal annotations, primarily through two kinds of temporal "containers". The first kind of container is the the relationship that each event has with the time of document creation (the DOCTIMEREL feature annotated in the first pass). The second source of "narrative container" annotation is a focus in the annotations on capturing temporal structure using CONTAINS (INCLUDES, in ISO-TimeML) relations between events and on capturing event-time relationships. This focus on temporal annotations can be measured directly – 40.7% of RED temporal relations are one of the two types of CONTAINS relations, whereas the equivalent relations in TimeBank 1.2 take up only 35% of the relations (using counts reported in (D'Souza and Ng, 2013)).

RED annotation expands upon that narrative container approach by adding subevent annotation. As with causal relations, it is noted that subevent relations also carry temporal information, and therefore they are captured by subtyping CONTAINS relations into two subtypes; purely temporal containment (CONTAINS), and a CONTAINS-SUBEVENT relation, which requires that the contained event be both spatiotemporally contained and also a subevent, being a part of the script or event structure of the larger event. When annotators agreed that two events were linked by some kind of CONTAINS relation, they agreed about distinction between CONTAINS and CONTAINS-SUBEVENT 90.2% of the time.

An outcome of this focus upon annotating both DOCTIMEREL, CONTAINS, and CONTAINS-SUBEVENT relations is a great deal of hierarchical temporal structure in a document, from which one may be able to infer the temporal relationship between two events purely through the temporal relationship of their narrative containers. RED expands upon that by adding event coreference, so that one may make temporal inference not just over a particular event mention, but all mentions of the same event. If one particular "chant" is part of a larger "protest" event, and the annotator knows that some mention of that "protest" is BEFORE a "speech" that instigates it, then the relationship between the "chant" and the "speech" can be viewed by annotators as inferrable, and therefore does not need to be annotated. RED guidelines furthermore limit BEFORE and OVERLAP relations to contexts in which the relation is perceived by an annotator to be explicitly expressed in the context. Section details more nuanced agreement results of temporal annotation.

### 3.4 Causal Annotation

Causation has often been divided into CAUSE, ENABLE and PREVENT, as outlined in Hobbs (2005) and Wolff (2007), and implemented in Mirza et al. (2014) and Mostafazadeh et al. (2016). RED annotation, based on preliminary studies of causal annotation in (Ikuta et al., 2014), adopted a two-way distinction between CAUSES and PRECONDITION similar to the distinction often made between "Cause" and "enable". RED represents "prevent" relations simply through polarity (being the cause or precondition for a negated event), which does re-

quire that all prevented events have a negated polarity. These CAUSES and PRECONDITION labels have been noted to generally combine with temporal information, and therefore annotators annotate causality with one of four fused labels: BEFORE/CAUSES, OVERLAP/CAUSES, BEFORE/PRECONDITION, and OVERLAP/PRECONDITION. This distinction has similarly been suggested in (Mostafazadeh et al., 2016), and bears practical similarity to the decisions in Hong et al. (2016) to allow multiple labels between two events, or the layered annotation of Mirza et al. (2014) on top of temporal structure.

This annotation aims towards logical definitions for cause and preconditions outlined in Ikuta et al (2014). This defines CAUSES as being true "if, according to the writer, the particular EVENT Y was inevitable given the particular EVENT X.", and PRECONDITION as being true when, "had the particular EVENT X not happened, the particular EVENT Y would not have happened.". Following (Bethard et al., 2008; Bethard, 2007; Prasad et al., 2008), those logical definitions were supplemented by guidelines for particular contexts, and for paraphrasing with particular implicit connectives, and case-by-case guideline for specific problematic frames, to handle edge cases which where challenging for classification by logical definition alone. Table 1 illustrates an example in which all four relations are illustrated:

*The **ouster** of Morsi and the subsequent **suppression** of the Brotherhood has **enraged** the groups members and led to a spate of scapegoating **attacks** by Muslim extremists*

**ouster** BEFORE/CAUSES **enrage**

**ouster** BEFORE/PRECONDITION **attacks**

**suppression** OVERLAP/CAUSE **enrage**

**suppression** OVERLAP/PRECONDITION **attacks**

**Figure 1:** An examples with the four causal types

### 3.5 Annotation Example

To give a summarizing sense of the output of the kind of annotation, we illustrate the culmination of the different layers of annotation with two sentences from the corpus. Figure 2 illustrates the relations annotated during the first pass, and which elements would be annotated as entities. Figure 3 illustrates the "events" which would be annotated in that first pass (which would also receive modality, polarity, relationship to document time, etc.) and the event-event relations annotated in a second pass.

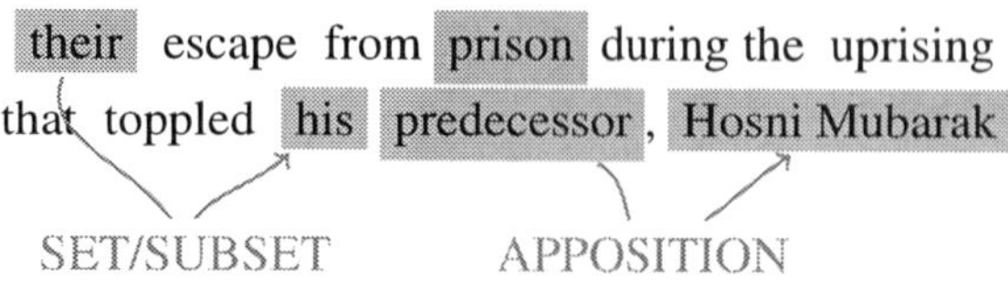


**Figure 2:** Example of entity annotation

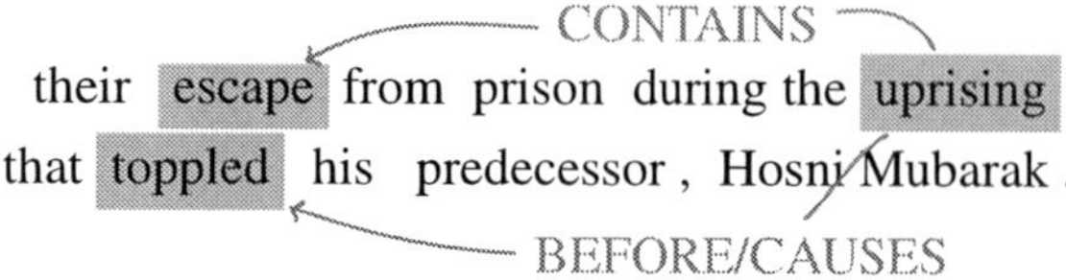


**Figure 3:** Example of event annotation pass

## 4   Annotation Analysis

### 4.1   Temporal Evaluation

We examine the relation agreement scores between annotators, and between annotators and the gold adjudicated data. While one might evaluate each relationship type – such as BEFORE/CAUSES – as an independent relation, that makes it difficult to compare this relationship annotation to prior endeavors, which have been focused upon temporal annotation tasks. Table 5 therefore also lists what the relation agreement would be if one were to remove causal and subevent relations (for example, treating BEFORE/CAUSES as BEFORE and CONTAINS-SUBEVENT as CONTAINS).

Those temporal relations can also be measured using the temporal closure evaluation method of Uzzaman et al. (2011), which proposes applying temporal closure to the reference (or in this case, gold) annotations when evaluating calculating precision, and apply temporal closure on the annotator annotations when calculating recall.

There have been suggestions for adapting the idea of closure to encompass making inference about other relations, as well. Glavas et al. (2014), for example, suggest that the subevent relation is transitive and should be measured with closure.

### 4.2   Locality and Density of Relation Annotations

Actual comparison of event corpora is made complicated by the wide variance in how many events (or relation-bearing predicates) are annotated per sentence, and how many relations are explicitly annotated, how many implicit relations are inferable, and the distance that is allowed when one makes an annotation. Annotation schemes such as Propbank (Palmer et al., 2005), FrameNet (Fillmore and Baker, 2000), Preposition annotation (Litkowski and Hargraves, 2005; Srikumar and Roth, 2013; Schneider et al., 2015) or AMR (Banarescu et al., 2013) have captured large quantities of temporal and causal relationships, but largely do so within very limited distances from a predicate. Other annotations such as PDTB (Prasad et al 2008) or RST (Carlson et al., 2003) may also capture relations, but are limited to adjacent sentences or adjacency pairs within rhetorical structure. However, there are plenty of contexts where an event may be clearly within a causal chain or an event-subevent relationship outside of such limited scopes.

Figure 4 shows the distance (in sentences) between events with various kinds of relations. One may see that CONTAINS-SUBEVENT relations have much more long-distance relations than terms. This is largely due to the nature of "subevent" relations, which can be annotated across many sentences, because the kind of world knowledge used to mark those relations is not reliant upon local words or constructions.

One may see that the RED annotation is far more dense, in having many event-event relations per event, and has a longer tail of long-distance relations for causal, contains and subevent relations. Indeed, roughly 18% of event chains have two or more relations (temporal, causal, subevent, or bridging) to other events or times. Figure 5 shows the distributions involved, and illustrates the natural idea that event coreference increases the number of event-event relations seen per event chain, and therefore the amount of contextual information about each event.

| Relation | count | inter-annotator | | | annotator against gold | | |
|---|---|---|---|---|---|---|---|
| | | F1 | Temp. only | +closure | F1 | temp. only | +closure |
| before | 609 | 23.2 | | | 60.9 | | |
| before/causes | 260 | 22.8 | 41.0 | 42.1 | 62.2 | 70.1 | 70.8 |
| before/precondition | 492 | 24.4 | | | 59.9 | | |
| overlap | 346 | 10.0 | | | 45.7 | | |
| overlap/causes | 221 | 26.2 | 20.6 | 22.2 | 59.8 | 54.4 | 55.2 |
| overlap/precondition | 174 | 4.9 | | | 46.7 | | |
| contains | 983 | 64.0 | 53.0 | 54.4 | 81.1 | 76.9 | 77.7 |
| contains-subevent | 729 | 25.8 | | | 66.7 | | |
| begins-on | 209 | 18.0 | 18.0 | 18.4 | 64.4 | 64.4 | 65.0 |
| ends-on | 138 | 28.3 | 28.3 | 28.3 | 69.2 | 69.2 | 69.2 |
| simultaneous | 57 | 0 | 0 | 0 | 43.5 | 43.5 | 43.5 |

**Table 5:** Agreement on event-event relations, and total corpus counts of each relation

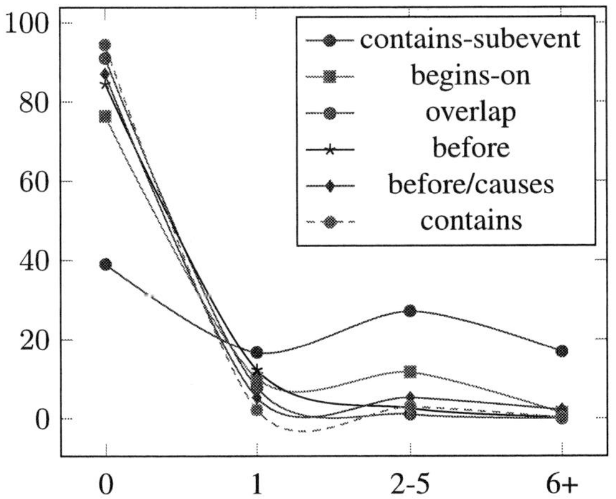

**Figure 4:** Distance between events, with 0 denoting within-sentence relations.

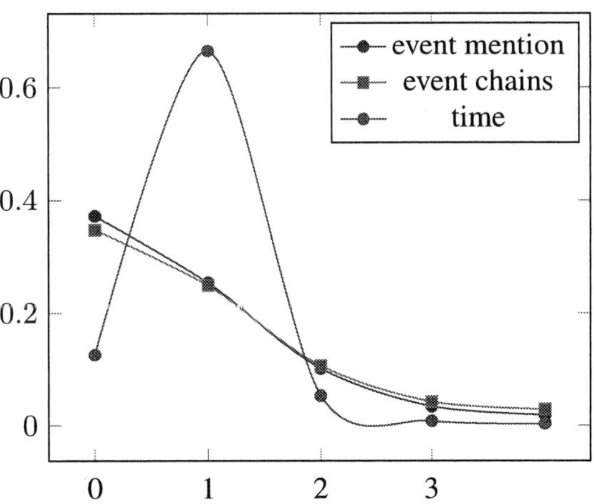

**Figure 5:** Relations per event, time, or event chain

## 4.3 Error Analysis of False Positive annotations

An ongoing issue with this annotation is whether annotators agree on which markables should be related. To explore these errors, we did a manual error analysis of relations discarded during adjudication. We randomly sampled 60 instances from the six relations constituting 87% of the errors (the two CONTAINS relation, the two PRECONDITION relations, and BEFORE and OVERLAP), and clustered them into kinds of issues, listed below:

**Presupposition(12)** : A particular edge case in RED causal relations are instances where annotators don't infer much of a causal link between events, but where event 2 definition-ally assumes event 1. One might have to get married once in order for later marriages to be called a "remarriage", for example, but many would hesistate to say that the marriage had a BEFORE/PRECONDITION relation to "re-marriage".

**Modality(8)** : Annotators disagreeing about relations that were ruled out due to different modalities or differing polarity of the events involved. We assume that most such errors are corrected in adjudication.

**Idiomatic(8)** : Annotators differing either in the exact interpretation of a complex temporal expression, or regarding the temporal structure implied by a particular multiword expression.

**Containment(6)** : Annotators who agree regarding whether two events are part of a larger structure of event-subevent relations or containment relations, but disagreed upon which event to attach to. Such relations are usually agreement under temporal closure.

**Inferrable(5)** : Temporal OVERLAP or BEFORE relations inferrable through document time, and which therefore did not require annotation.

**Resultatives(4)** : Interpretations of whether the temporal spans of events such as "injured" or "encouraged" refer to the state of being injured/encouraged or to the precipitating event.

**Other(17)**

## 5   Conclusion

This paper presents a set of guidelines for annotating causality, temporal relations, subevent relations, coreference and bridging coreference, and presents evaluations of the quality of these annotations. While the individual kinds of phenomena annotated in this corpus have been studied before, such relations have not been annotated together in the same datasets.

We also note that the details of this annotation are similar to other recently developed corpora, perhaps signaling that parallel work in this area may be trending towards a consensus. One such point can be seen in similar treatments of how causal and temporal links are annotated. Both this work and the CaTeRS corpus (Mostafazadeh et al., 2016) adopt very similar treatments of causality, in which the temporal and causal links are joined together into links such as BEFORE/CAUSES. Work such as Mira et al. (2014), while annotating causal relations separately from TimeBank temporal links, have focused upon learning the relationships between causal and temporal structure.

It is hoped that such a richly annotated corpus can provide the opportunity for joint learning that may not be viable with existing corpora. The described corpus will be released, and the guidelines are publicly available. While it remains the case that no singular corpus has become a standardized benchmark for the development of many of these relations, we hope that the current work may help move the community further towards general annotation and prediction of event coreference, representation and

event-event relations, and that it may shed light upon the utility of annotating many kinds of event phenomena over the same corpus.

## Acknowledgments

We thank the DEFT - FA-8750-13-2-0045 via a subcontract from LDC, and thank the LDC for cooperation in obtaining and distributing the source material. We also thank members of the DEFT Events Workshop community and three anonymous reviewers for feedback regarding the guidelines and paper. Any opinions, findings, and conclusions or recommendations expressed in this material are those of the authors and do not necessarily reflect the views of DARPA or the US government.

## References

Laura Banarescu, Claire Bonial, Shu Cai, Madalina Georgescu, Kira Griffitt, Ulf Hermjakob, Kevin Knight, Philipp Koehn, Martha Palmer, and Nathan Schneider. 2013. Abstract meaning representation for sembanking. In *Proc. of the Linguistic Annotation Workshop and Interoperability with Discourse*.

Steven Bethard, William J Corvey, Sara Klingenstein, and James H Martin. 2008. Building a Corpus of Temporal-Causal Structure. In *LREC*.

Steven John Bethard. 2007. *Finding event, temporal and causal structure in text: A machine learning approach.*

Lynn Carlson, Daniel Marcu, and Mary Ellen Okurowski. 2003. Building a discourse-tagged corpus in the framework of rhetorical structure theory. In *Current and new directions in discourse and dialogue*, pages 85–112. Springer.

Herbert H Clark. 1975. Bridging. In *Proceedings of the 1975 workshop on Theoretical issues in natural language processing*, pages 169–174. Association for Computational Linguistics.

Agata Cybulska and Piek Vossen. 2014. Using a sledgehammer to crack a nut? Lexical diversity and event coreference resolution. In *LREC*, pages 4545–4552.

Jennifer D'Souza and Vincent Ng. 2013. Classifying temporal relations with rich linguistic knowledge. In *HLT-NAACL*, pages 918–927.

Jesse Dunietz, Lori Levin, and Jaime Carbonell. 2015. Annotating Causal Language Using Corpus Lexicography of Constructions. In *The 9th Linguistic Annotation Workshop held in conjuncion with NAACL 2015*, page 188.

Charles J. Fillmore and Collin F. Baker. 2000. FrameNet: Frame Semantics Meets the Corpus. In *Poster presentation, 74th Annual Meeting of the Linguistic Society of America*, January.

Goran Glava and Jan najder. 2014. Constructing Coherent Event Hierarchies from News Stories. *TextGraphs-9*, page 34.

Goran Glava, Jan Snajder, Parisa Kordjamshidi, and Marie-Francine Moens. 2014. HiEve: A Corpus for Extracting Event Hierarchies from News Stories. In *Proceedings of 9th language resources and evaluation conference*.

Jerry R Hobbs. 2005. Toward a useful concept of causality for lexical semantics. *Journal of Semantics*, 22(2):181–209.

Yu Hong, Tongtao Zhang, Sharone Horowit-Hendler, Heng Ji, Tim O'Gorman, and Martha Palmer. 2016. Building a Cross-document Event-Event Relation Corpus. In *Proceedings of LREC 2016*.

Rei Ikuta, William F. Styler IV, Mariah Hamang, Tim OGorman, and Martha Palmer. 2014. Challenges of Adding Causation to Richer Event Descriptions. *Proceedings of the 2nd Workshop on Events*, page 12.

Jonathan K Kummerfeld and Dan Klein. 2013. Error-driven analysis of challenges in coreference resolution. In *Proceedings of the 2013 Conference on Empirical Methods in Natural Language Processing, Seattle, Wash*, pages 18–21.

Heeyoung Lee, Marta Recasens, Angel Chang, Mihai Surdeanu, and Dan Jurafsky. 2012. Joint entity and event coreference resolution across documents. In *Proceedings of the 2012 Joint Conference on Empirical Methods in Natural Language Processing and Computational Natural Language Learning*, pages 489–500. Association for Computational Linguistics.

Shasha Liao and Ralph Grishman. 2010. Using document level cross-event inference to improve event extraction. In *Proceedings of the 48th Annual Meeting of the Association for Computational Linguistics*, pages 789–797. Association for Computational Linguistics.

Kenneth C Litkowski and Orin Hargraves. 2005. The preposition project. In *Proceedings of the Second ACL-SIGSEM Workshop on the Linguistic Dimensions of Prepositions and their Use in Computational Linguistics Formalisms and Applications*, pages 171–179.

Anne-Lyse Minard, Manuela Speranza, Ruben Urizar, Begona Altuna, Marieke van Erp, Anneleen Schoen, and Chantal van Son. 2016. MEANTIME, the NewsReader multilingual event and time corpus. *Proceedings of LREC2016*.

Paramita Mirza, Rachele Sprugnoli, Sara Tonelli, and Manuela Speranza. 2014. Annotating causality in the TempEval-3 corpus. In *Proceedings of the EACL 2014 Workshop on Computational Approaches to Causality in Language (CAtoCL)*, pages 10–19.

Nasrin Mostafazadeh, Alyson Grealish, Nathanael Chambers, James Allen, and Lucy Vanderwende. 2016. CaTeRS: Causal and Temporal Relation Scheme for Semantic Annotation of Event Structures. In *Proceedings of the 4th Workshop on Events*.

M. Palmer, P. Kingsbury, and D. Gildea. 2005. The proposition bank: An annotated corpus of semantic roles. *Computational Linguistics*, 31(1):71–106.

Haoruo Peng, Kai-Wei Chang, and Dan Roth. 2015. A joint framework for coreference resolution and mention head detection. *CoNLL 2015*, 51:12.

Massimo Poesio, Renata Vieira, and Simone Teufel. 1997. Resolving bridging references in unrestricted text. In *Proceedings of a Workshop on Operational Factors in Practical, Robust Anaphora Resolution for Unrestricted Texts*, pages 1–6. Association for Computational Linguistics.

Sameer Pradhan, Xiaoqiang Luo, Marta Recasens, Eduard Hovy, Vincent Ng, and Michael Strube. 2014.

Scoring coreference partitions of predicted mentions: A reference implementation. In *Proceedings of the 52nd Annual Meeting of the Association for Computational Linguistics (Short Papers)*, pages 30–35.

Rashmi Prasad, Nikhil Dinesh, Alan Lee, Eleni Miltsakaki, Livio Robaldo, Aravind K Joshi, and Bonnie L Webber. 2008. The Penn Discourse TreeBank 2.0. In *LREC*. Citeseer.

J. Pustejovsky and A. Stubbs. 2011. Increasing informativeness in temporal annotation. In *ACL HLT 2011*, page 152.

James Pustejovsky, Jos M Castano, Robert Ingria, Roser Sauri, Robert J Gaizauskas, Andrea Setzer, Graham Katz, and Dragomir R Radev. 2003. TimeML: Robust specification of event and temporal expressions in text. *New directions in question answering*, 3:28–34.

Mehwish Riaz and Roxana Girju. 2013. Toward a better understanding of causality between verbal events: Extraction and analysis of the causal power of verb-verb associations. In *Proceedings of the annual SIGdial Meeting on Discourse and Dialogue (SIGDIAL)*.

Nathan Schneider, Vivek Srikumar, Jena D Hwang, and Martha Palmer. 2015. A hierarchy with, of, and for preposition supersenses. In *The 9th Linguistic Annotation Workshop held in conjuncion with NAACL 2015*, page 112.

Zhiyi Song, Ann Bies, Stephanie Strassel, Tom Riese, Justin Mott, Joe Ellis, Jonathan Wright, Seth Kulick, Neville Ryant, and Xiaoyi Ma. 2015. From light to rich ere: annotation of entities, relations, and events. In *Proceedings of the 3rd Workshop on EVENTS at the NAACL-HLT*, pages 89–98.

Vivek Srikumar and Dan Roth. 2013. Modeling semantic relations expressed by prepositions. *Transactions of the Association for Computational Linguistics*, 1:231–242.

William F. Styler IV, Steven Bethard, Sean Finan, Martha Palmer, Sameer Pradhan, Piet C. de Groen, Brad Erickson, Timothy Miller, Chen Lin, Guergana Savova, and others. 2014. Temporal annotation in the clinical domain. *Transactions of the Association for Computational Linguistics*, 2:143–154.

Naushad UzZaman and James F Allen. 2011. Temporal evaluation. In *Proceedings of the 49th Annual Meeting of the Association for Computational Linguistics: Human Language Technologies: short papers-Volume 2*, pages 351–356. Association for Computational Linguistics.

Piek Vossen, Tommaso Caselli, and Yiota Kontzopoulou. 2015. Storylines for structuring massive streams of news. In *Proceedings of the First Workshop on Computing News Storylines*, pages 40–49.

Ralph Weischedel, Eduard Hovy, Mitchell Marcus, Martha Palmer, Robert Belvin, Sameer Pradhan, Lance Ramshaw, and Nianwen Xue. 2011. OntoNotes: A large training corpus for enhanced processing. *Handbook of Natural Language Processing and Machine Translation. Springer.*

# NASTEA: Investigating Narrative Schemas through Annotated Entities


**Dan Simonson**
Department of Linguistics
Georgetown University
Washington, DC 20057
des62@georgetown.edu

**Anthony Davis**
Ashland, OR 97520
tonydavis0@gmail.com


## Abstract


In this paper, we investigate the distribution of narrative schemas (Chambers and Jurafsky, 2009) throughout different document categories and how the structure of narrative schemas is conditioned by document category, the converse of the relationship explored in Simonson and Davis (2015). We evaluate cross-category narrative differences by assessing the predictability of verbs in each category and the salience of arguments to events that narrative schemas highlight. For the former, we use the *narrative cloze* task employed in previous work on schemas. For the latter, we introduce a task that employs narrative schemas called *narrative argument salience through entities annotated*, or *NASTEA*. We compare the schemas induced from the entire corpus to those from the subcorpora for each topic using these two types of evaluation. Results of each evaluation vary by each topical subcorpus, in some cases showing improvement, but the NASTEA task additionally reveals that some the documents within some topics are significantly more rigid in their narrative structure, instantiating a limited number of schemas in a highly predictable fashion.


## 1 Introduction

A number of approaches for detecting narrative structures in text have been devised in recent years. Drawing from the work of Schank and Abelson (1977) and subsequent efforts to automatically populate templates with specific events and particpants referred to in text, Chambers and Jurafsky (2008; 2009) created the first statistically induced versions of such models. Chambers and Jurafsky (2008) described a basic version of their approach, in which single narrative chains involving a participant are generated; Chambers and Jurafsky (2009) builds on that work to create entire *narrative schemas*—generalized story lines that contain events and chains of potential role fillers that span across events. Other models have been devised for analyzing narrative (Vossen et al., 2015; Miller et al., 2015), but we will employ a variant of Chambers and Jurafsky (2009)'s narrative model in this work.

Chambers and Jurafsky (2008; 2009) introduced the narrative cloze task for evaluating their results. This involves removing a single word from a narrative chain in a held out document; the language model must then predict the missing word. The model is scored by how highly it ranks the true hidden word compared to all other possible replacements. A number of generative models have been introduced to further improve performance on cloze, and have done so successfully (Jans et al. 2012; Cheung et al., 2013; Chambers, 2013; Pichotta and Mooney 2014; Nguyen et al. 2015). More recently, it has been shown that a LSTM recurrent neural network can improve performance as well (Pichotta and Mooney 2015). These models focus on improving performance on the narrative cloze. Typically, they use the ordering of words in a chain as a factor, endowing them with the ability to anticipate the linguistic structure of the documents they model, but less able to produce schemas that represent conventionalized narrative structures. For instance, a model of news text that guesses the widespread, nonspecific verb "say" may perform well on narrative cloze,




*Proceedings of 2nd Workshop on Computing News Storylines*, pages 57–66,
Austin, TX, November 5, 2016. ©2016 Association for Computational Linguistics

but such a model is unlikely to reveal the world knowledge forming part of a conventionalized sequence of events.

Thus in some ways, while recent work has succeeded in raising the bar for solving the cloze task, it has sidestepped the original goal, which was to act as "a comparative measure to evaluate narrative knowledge" (Chambers, 2011, 26 – 27). Conservative guesses on narrative cloze alone create strong linguistic templates but poor narratological ones. Two issues raise concerns about the value of cloze as an evaluation of the narrative aspect of schemas. First, the focus on statistical associations between verbs misses a key component of narrative, namely, the connections between participants common to the events within a narrative, which establish it as a coherent narrative in the first place. Second, these measures of statistical association will make it clear which types of actions tend to be mentioned in concert within a document, but they may be less successful in detecting associations between participants in those events, for at least two reasons: there are many more participants (e.g., named individuals) referred to in a corpus than there are verbs, and there are various ways of referring to the same participant within the course of a narrative (e.g., different name strings, descriptions, titles, and pronouns).

Additionally, little work has been done exploring the properties of Chambers' narrative schemas. Simonson and Davis (2015) attempt to determine whether the events in narrative schemas can be used as especially sensitive features for a naïve Bayes classifier. They demonstrate that schema events alone do not seem to predict document category (e.g. $schemas \not\to category$) However, they do not demonstrate the converse, whether constraining document category can produce better schemas (e.g. $category \to schemas?$), which we will attempt to show here.

In this study, we intend to explore the properties of narrative schemas by investigating the influence of document category on schemas generated. Intuitively, detecting narrative sequences of events and their participants in text seems important, and the ability, e.g., to automatically generate as well as populate such schemas or templates is one clear application of this line of research. However, evaluation of schemas on this and similar tasks is not straightforward, as a gold standard is not clearly defined. We discuss and compare two techniques that are readily implemented and for which a gold standard is available: *narrative cloze* and *NASTEA*, an entity extraction task. NASTEA's reliance on schemas should add more transparency to the evaluation process, with schemas providing clear representations of patterns at the discourse level.

In Section (2), we will describe in detail the prior schema generation work we will modify for looking at topical conditioning. In Section (3), we describe our dataset. In Section (4), we describe our modifications of prior work for generating schemas. In Section (5), we describe in detail the NASTEA task we used to investigate schemas in this paper. In Section (6), we describe our results, followed by discussion (Section 7) and conclusions (Section 8).

## 2  Chambers and Jurafsky's Schema Model

In this paper, we work with Chambers and Jurafsky (2009)'s $pmi$-based narrative schemas, using a nearly identical score and generation procedure, though with a different data set and some extensions to explore the role of topic in a schema-learning procedure. These changes will be discussed in Section (4); here we will discuss the original model.

Fundamentally, Chambers and Jurafsky (2009) consider the problem of how well a new verb-dependency pair $\langle f, g \rangle$ fits into a chain of an existing schema, where $f$ is some verb and $g$ is a dependency. This relationship is defined in Equation (1) as $chainsim'$:

$$chainsim'(C, \langle f, g \rangle) =$$
$$\max_a \left( score(C, a) + \sum_{i=1}^{n} sim(\langle e_i, d_i \rangle, \langle f, g \rangle, a) \right)$$
$$(1)$$

There are two main components of note here: $score(C, a)$, which assesses how well an argument type $a$ fits in with chain $C$ and $\sum_{i=1}^{n} sim(\langle e_i, d_i \rangle, \langle f, g \rangle, a)$, which determines how well the new pair $\langle f, g \rangle$ fits in with the rest of the existing chain, given argument type $a$.

*score* is defined as:

$$score(C, a) = \sum_{i=1}^{n-1} \sum_{j=i+1}^{n} sim(\langle e_i, d_i \rangle, \langle e_j, d_j \rangle, a) \tag{2}$$

which checks, for every pair in $C$, the compatability of argument $a$. Both of these depend on $sim$, which is defined as:

$$sim(\langle e, d \rangle, \langle e', d' \rangle, a) =$$
$$pmi(\langle e, d \rangle, \langle e', d' \rangle) + \lambda \log freq(\langle e, d \rangle, \langle e', d' \rangle, a) \tag{3}$$

$sim$ establishes the relationship between two verb/dependency pairs $\langle e, d \rangle$ and $\langle e', d' \rangle$ on two different levels: the $pmi$ establishes their general strength through coreference; if a verb/dependency pair shares a coreferring argument with another verb/dependency pair, this counts toward increasing the joint probability used in computing the pointwise mutual information between the two. $\lambda \log freq(\langle e, d \rangle, \langle e', d' \rangle, a)$ defines the strength of that connection with argument $a$ in the mix, with the $freq$ being the counts of $\langle e, d \rangle$ and $\langle e', d' \rangle$ appearing together with a shared argument $a$.

## 3  Data

Our data comes from the New York Times corpus (Sandhaus 2008), a corpus containing 1.8 million articles from the New York Times from January 1987 to June 2007. Each article is annotated with metadata, including document categories—for our purposes, the `online producer` tag in the New York Times corpus—and salient entity annotations—people, organizations, and locations. Each article has been human-annotated with extensive metadata, including document categories—for our purposes, the `online producer` tag—and salient entity annotations—people, organizations, and locations.

To investigate our research question, we select a subset of document categories in the corpus that appear with a similar frequency and represent a broad range of topics (Table 1). The schemas used in this study are induced from this set of documents. In one procedure, the entire set of documents serves as the corpus for a single set of schemas. In a second, we create a topic-specific set of schemas, using the set of documents assigned to a given topic as the corpus for a set of schemas. One aim of this is to investigate the extent to which evaluation measures are affected by topic specificity. A second is to examine how the sets of topic-specific schemas might differ.

**Table 1:** Counts of document categories selected from the `online producer` tag for use in this study. Frequencies vary, but were chosen to be around the same order of magnitude and to represent different sorts of topics.

| `online producer` category | counts |
| --- | --- |
| Law and Legislation | 52110 |
| Weddings and Engagements | 51195 |
| Crime and Criminals | 50981 |
| United States Armament and Defense | 50642 |
| Computers and the Internet | 49413 |
| Labor | 46321 |
| Top/News/Obituaries | 36360 |

Once the documents of these categories were extracted, they were pre-processed using Stanford CoreNLP (Manning et al. 2014). Of particular importance are the Stanford Parser (de Marneffe et al. 2006) and `dcoref` (Lee et al. 2013), used for coreference resolution. These play a central role in the schema generation process described in the next section. Documents where parsing or coreference failed to complete were removed from processing as well.

## 4  Modifications to Schema Generation

We now briefly discuss our modifications to Chambers and Jurafsky (2009)'s schema generation technique, described in detail in Section (2). Our model varies fundamentally from Chambers and Jurafsky (2009)'s in that it is conditioned by document category, in this case selected from the `online producer` categories from the NYT corpus that we were interested in. Separate models are trained for each document category, only on documents contained in that category. The only exception to this is the baseline model, which is trained on all documents into one single model. We surmise that the resulting schemas should be "more topic-specific" than those generated by the baseline model, which lumps all topics together.

Conditioning schema generation by document category, as noted above, is one key difference. Additionally, there are a few small changes at some of the post-score steps in the procedure. The score value from Chambers and Jurafsky (2009) does not explicitly describe how a newly added event's argument slots should be tied to the existing chains in the schema it is being added to. We handle this in a separate step—after it is decided that an event should be added to a schema, connections are made at that point where the threshold can be crossed. Also, we allow for an event to be added to multiple schemas if the score is high enough. In part, this is to allow for the words meaning to be captured across multiple contexts.

Lastly, we genericize some types—similar to Balsubramanian et al. (2013)—but not in all circumstances; instead, we do so only in the event that there is no common noun available to learn from. Our algorithm first checks the Stanford NER (Finkel et al. 2005) to see if there are any available types. Then it checks if there are any pronouns in the chain, and attempts to guess a type for the chain based on that. Finally, if there are no other types available, it aborts to a fallback type.

During the process of generation, a random selection of 10% of documents were held out for evaluation.

Figure (1) depicts a schema generated by our procedure.

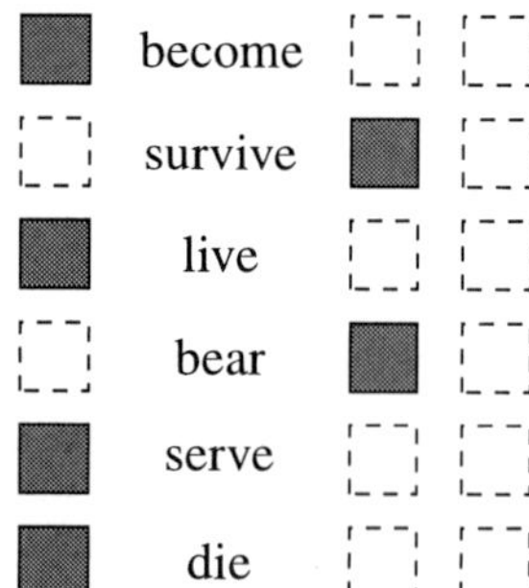


**Figure 1:** A relatively simple schema from the *Top/News/Obituaries* document category. The red squares indicate a chain that is strongly represented by the generic type PERSON, but with many other lionizing human types: scholar, hero, advocate, philosopher, etc. The dashed squares represent slots attested in the data but not connected during schema generation. In other words, this schema contains a single chain such that: PERSON/hero/advocate was born, lived, served, became, died, and was survived by...

## 5 Narrative Argument Salience Through Entities Annotated (NASTEA)

In this section, we will describe our technique for evaluating schemas using annotated entities.

Any evaluation applied to narrative schemas implicitly defines the notion of narrative. Since there are many aspects of the somewhat vague concept of narrative, and since, as noted above, there is no single obvious and clearly defined task and gold standard for evaluation of narrative schemas, a single type of evaluation is unlikely to gauge all of these aspects adequately. To address some of these shortcomings, we propose a task that is solvable, evaluates schemas directly, and concerns an aspect of narrative orthogonal to what the cloze task involves—the participants. Salient entity annotations in the New York Times corpus, performed by trained human indexers, appear well suited to this task. We investigate whether we can use narrative schemas to identify these salient entities, under the assumption that entities deemed important by the annotators indicate *Narrative Argument Salience Through Entities Annotated*, or *NASTEA*.

There are three steps of the NASTEA task that must be described in detail. First, in Section (5.1), we describe the notion of the *presence* of a schema in a document. Second, in Section (5.2), we describe how a present schema is used to extract salient entities from a text, and how those extractions are scored against the gold standard. Finally, in Section (5.3), we describe how this procedure is executed using an arbitrary number of schemas to produce curves indicating the performance of a group of schemas of the NASTEA task.

### 5.1 Identifying a Schema in a Document

Determining whether or not a word or n-gram appears in a document is a relatively simple task, but identifying whether a narrative schema is present or not is neither trivial nor categorical. In this study, we deploy a measure of *presence* that reflects the *canonicality* of a document—that is, how closely a document matches a schema. This measure uses the events of a schema as a proxy for its content—excluding the arguments from the measure. We explicitly exclude coreference information from the measure since coreference is error prone; while we

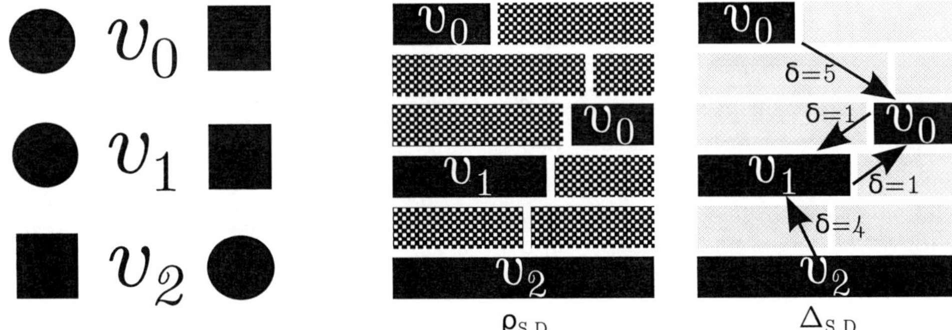

**Figure 2:** An illustration of how the presence $p_{S,D}$ (Formula 6) of a schema $S$ (left) is measured with respect to a document $D$ (both center and right). Each of the two illustrations of $D$ shows how the document appears with respect to the respective measure: density $\rho_{S,D}$ (Formula 4) in the center and dispersion $\Delta_{S,D}$ (Formula 5) to the right. In this example, $\rho_{S,D}$ is 4/11; $\Delta_{S,D}$ is $1/4 \times (5 + 1 + 1 + 4) = 11/4$; $p_{S,D}$ is $4^2/11^2$.

trust it en masse for generalizing over many documents, we are not so sure coreference can be trusted while considering one single document.

Measuring the presence $p_{S,D}$ of a schema $S$ in a document $D$ begins with $V_{S,D}$, the set of tokens from $D$ that represent events in $S$. The same token type can appear multiple times in the set as long as multiple tokens of it appear throughout $D$. A sentence can have multiple verbs, and all relevant verbs are included in $V_{S,D}$.

There are two ways to consider the distribution of verbs within a document, both of which we want to contribute to defining presence: *density* and *dispersion*. Density $\rho$ is defined as:

$$\rho_{S,D} = \frac{|V_{S,D}|}{|D|} \qquad (4)$$

where $|D|$ is the number of sentences in the document, and $V_{S,D}$ is defined above. In other words, $\rho_{S,D}$ measures how much of the document $D$ is composed of verbs $V_{S,D}$ representing the events in schema $S$. If this factor is high, then the document as a whole is very close to being only the series of events expressed in relevant schema. This is illustrated in the centered $\rho_{S,D}$ component of Figure (2)—the full black segments of $\rho$ illustration represent members of $V_{S,D}$, the checker-patterned components represent sentences that do not contain any members of $V_{S,D}$.

While a high density value is a strong indicator of presence, some cases where the density is not as high may still be interesting. We hypothesize that verbs belonging to a schema appearing close together probably indicate an expression of that schema, while the same verbs more widely dispersed in the document are less likely to instantiate it. We therefore define the dispersion $\Delta_{S,D}$ with respect to a schema $S$ and a document $D$ as:

$$\Delta_{S,D} = \frac{1}{|V_{S,D}|} \sum_{v_i \in V_{S,D}} \min_{v_j \in V_{S,D} - \{v_i\}} \delta(v_i, v_j) \qquad (5)$$

where $\delta(v_i, v_j)$ indicates the distance in sentences between two verbs $v_i$ and $v_j$. The minimization seeks to find the nearest $v_j$ to $v_i$ in $V_{S,D}$, which is computed for every $v_i$ contained in $V_{S,D}$. This is illustrated in Figure (2) as well, on the far right. Each arrow points from a specific $v_i$ to the specific $v_j$ where the distance is smallest.

The presence measure should be higher for those documents in which the elements of a schema are both dense (throughout the document) and not dispersed, so we define *canonical presence $p$* as:

$$p_{S,D} = \frac{\rho_{S,D}}{\Delta_{S,D}} \qquad (6)$$

This defines the extent to which a schema is present in a document—more specifically, the degree to which a document itself comes close to being an exemplar of the schema. The components of $p$ are illustrated in Figure (2).

## 5.2 Extracting Salient Entities with a Schema

Once schemas have been ranked for presence, they must be applied to a document in some way. We use the verb/dependency pairs found in that document that are also present in a schema to extract entities of importance. From each pair, any NP governed through the indicated dependency is extracted in whole. Only NPs containing proper nouns (/NNP.*/) are retained, as common nouns are not indicated in the NYT Metadata.

One side effect of Chambers' algorithm is a large number of schemas containing only a single verb—having only weak connections with the events in any other schema. We excluded these schemas from the NASTEA task.

The entities extracted are compared with the entities indicated in the NYT Metadata, a union of the `person`, `organization`, and `location` tags for each document. Each person, organization, or location from the metadata is tokenized with NLTK's (Bird et al. 2009) `wordpuncttokenizer` and is normalized for capitalization. Punctuation tokens are removed. Each entity extracted from the data is considered equal to the metadata entity if a fraction of the tokens $r$ are equal between the two. This $r$ value is set at 0.2, which is quite low, but justifiable, as any overlap between the open-class proper noun components likely indicates a match expressed differently from the normalized representation in the metadata: for example, an extraction of "Mr. Clinton" should match "William Jefferson Clinton" in the metadata. A higher threshold would have excluded these sorts of matches, which are typical of the writing style of the New York Times but differ in their metadata.

The fraction of entities from the metadata captured represents the *recall* while the fraction of things extracted actually found in the metadata indicates *precision*. NASTEA scores are reported as the F1 score of both of these values.

## 5.3 NASTEA Curves and Their Interpretation

As much as we would wish for it to be the case, the most present schema does not always yield the correct entities. In many cases, adding additional schemas of high presence is required. We use a set of schemas for each document, increasing this quan-

tity by groups of five, starting at one. This allows us to see how well the first schema applied performed, followed by the the top 6, followed by the top 11, etc. If only the highest presence schema is applied, then that is expressed as "$N_1$;" for the top 6, that is reported as "$N_6$," etc. Nevertheless, $N_1$ results are of particular interest to us—this is the "I'm feeling lucky" narrative schema, the one with the highest presence with respect to a document. The $N_1$ performance should be highest in documents where canonicality most strongly applies.

We split the data by document category, then generated schemas for each category. In evaluation, only schemas generated with documents from a specific category were applied to that specific category. Analogously, this was done for the narrative cloze task, but instead of schemas, each model—learned from the documents in that one single category—was applied to predict events for that specific category. In both experiments, documents that were members of multiple categories, about 9% of the held-out 27498 documents, were removed from the hold-out data to remove any possible penalties due to categorical overlap.

# 6 Results

Table 2: Average rank of answers in the narrative cloze.

| Test Model | Avg. Rank |
|---|---|
| Baseline | 1329 |
| Topical | 1273 |
| Top/News/Obituaries | 565 |
| Weddings and Engagements | 1058 |
| Law and Legislation | 1279 |
| Labor | 1297 |
| Crime and Criminals | 1268 |
| Computers and the Internet | 1346 |
| United States Armament and Defense | 1805 |

Of the narrative schemas generated,[1] around 13% were shared between document categories on average. Each categorical set of schemas shares around 26% of its schemas with the baseline set.

---

[1] The schemas are available for download at `http://schemas.thedansimonson.com`.

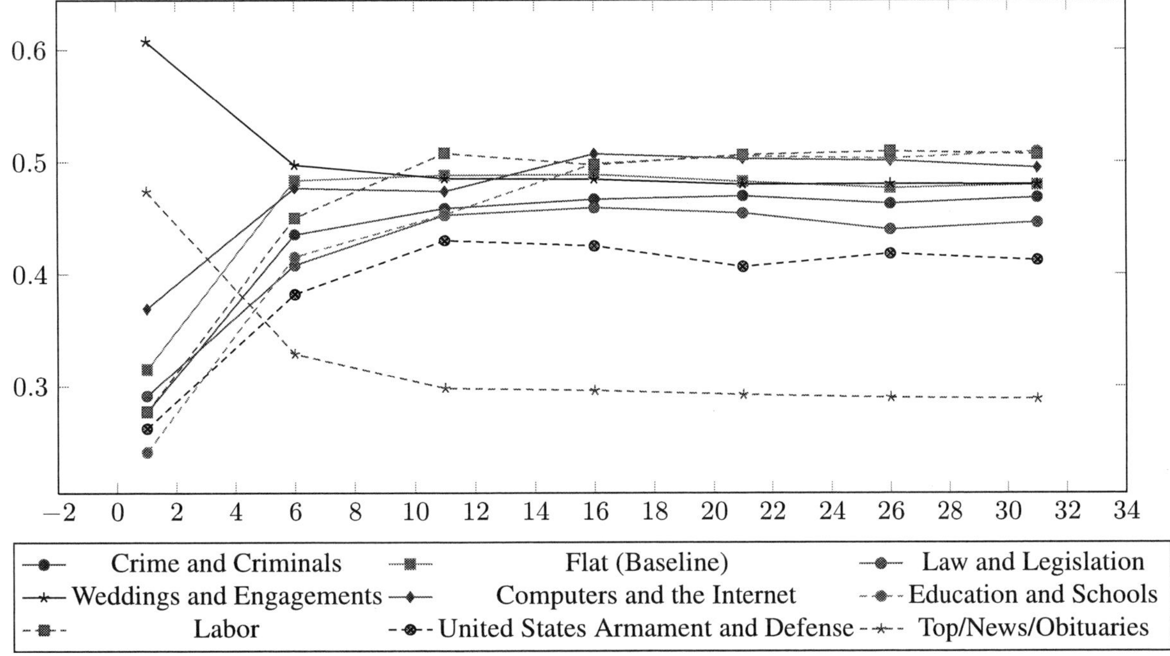

**Figure 3:** Plot of test-by-test performance on the NASTEA task for each topic. The $x$-axis indicates number of top-$n$ present schemas applied. The $y$-axis indicates F1 score (i.e. $N_n$) on the number of entities retrieved by the set of top-$n$ schemas.

Table (2) contains the cloze task results. Figure (3) illustrates results for the NASTEA task, broken down by document category. Most categories follow a general trend of performing poorly with the highest-presence guess alone. As more schemas are applied, the system is better able to retrieve annotated entities on most categories, with F1-scores leveling off around 45%. These values remain more or less stable *ad infinitum* with a few minor variations in value as $n$ continues to increase. The "flat" baseline model follows this trend adequately as well.

However, two categories are exceptions to this trend: *Weddings and Engagements* and *Top/News/Obituaries*. Their $N_1$ performances are significantly[2] higher than their counterparts' scores, and their curves are concave up. This difference is supported by the results of the cloze task as well.[3]

This exceptional $N_1$ performance invites closer inspection, which can be seen in Figure (4). Since NASTEA is applying schemas to documents, those schemas can be retained and counted allowing for

illustration of the variety of different schemas that seem to best fit a particular document, what we will refer to as *narrative homogeneity*. Figure (4) takes the $N_1$ results and illustrates the totals of counts for schemas that were applied in each $N_1$ case. Categories that performed well on $N_1$ were also more homogeneous at $N_1$, choosing a single schema as most present more often than their more heterogeneous counterparts.

## 7 Discussion

The NASTEA task shows a clear, discrete distinction between two types of document categories: those that seem to be narratologically homogeneous and others that seem to be narratologically heterogeneous within the scope of this model of narrative. In the homogeneous case, the assertion that $category \rightarrow schema$ seems to be valid, while in more heterogeneous circumstances, this is much less the case. This affirms Miller et. al. (2015)'s observation that their own corpus is characterized by a "heterogeneity of the articles' foci," with their corpus likely fitting into the *United States Armament and Defense* category—a notably heteroge-

---

[2]$p < 0.001$ including the baseline with the heterogeneous categories; $p < 0.005$ excluding the baseline from the analysis.
[3]$p < 0.05$

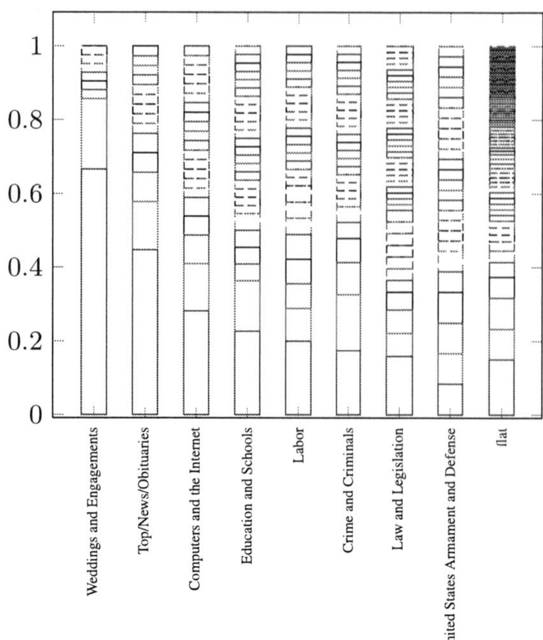

**Figure 4:** Plot of $N_1$ Document Categorical Narrative Homogeneity: A representation of the fractional distribution of schemas with the highest presence across all documents in a category ($n = 1$ for the NASTEA task). The y-axis Each slice of the whole indicates the fraction of a single schema having the highest presence for a document. A larger slice indicates that the single schema it represents had the highest presence for more documents in that topic than a smaller slice.

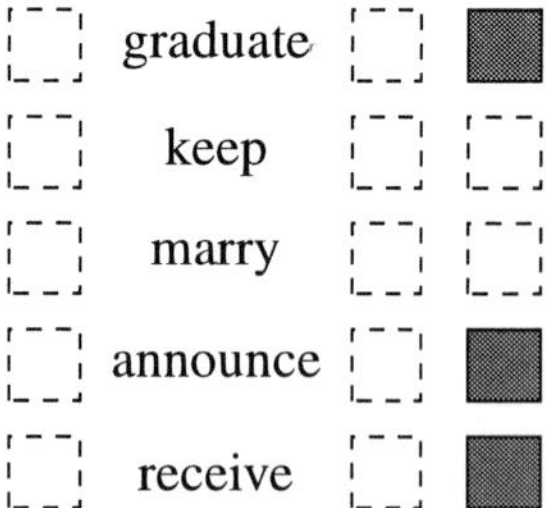



**Figure 5:** Schema generated in the *Weddings* document category. The dashed squares represent slots attested in the data but not connected during schema generation. The chain of red squares indicates a generic organization type. The other slots remain largely unlinked because they are frequently found as conjunctive arguments of reciprocal verbs the are not handled well by the existing narrative models.

neous one—were it derived from the NYT Corpus.

Of those we used in this study, the *Weddings and Engagements* and *Top/News/Obituaries* (referred to hereafter as *Weddings* and *Obituaries*, respectively) are distinctly homogeneous. This distinction is reaffirmed through the cloze task as well, where each of their respective rank averages are hundreds of ranks higher. This indicates that they are more rigid in their choice of wording and the events they describe, and those events point more strictly toward the entities the NYT library scientists annotated. It is not too surprising that these particular categories are different. Impressionistically, the writing styles of such documents are more rigid than their more news-typical counterparts. However, the objective measurability of this impression via two distinct forms of evaluation is a first.

There are two possible interpretations of this result. One is that the homogeneous categories are truly something different from the heterogeneous ones, and that this is a fact about news narratives and document categories at large. This is very much plausible, as *Weddings* and *Obituaries* are categories defined by the events contained within them: marriage and death, and the events that lead up to those. Events in *United States Armament and Defense* can vary dramatically: from roadside bombings to budget overruns. The other interpretation is that the homogeneous categories are ones that are better encapsulated by our model of narratives and that the heterogeneous ones are not captured properly. This makes the NASTEA task something to optimize performance on, making it a quantitative metric for evaluating improvements in narrative schemas. These are not necessarily contradictory interpretations if one accepts both of them as independently representing different aspects of the notion of narrative.

While cloze and NASTEA overall agreed on the exceptionality of *Weddings* and *Obituaries*, there remain some discrepancies between the two. *Obituaries* performs much better on cloze relative to *Weddings*, while on NASTEA, the reverse happens, and *Weddings* outperforms *Obituaries*. Within the rest of the categories, rankings shuffle around between the two. For example, *Computers and the Internet* performed well below average on cloze, but ranked third highest on $N_1$, with the homogeneity to match.

Narrative cloze's opacity makes these discrepancies difficult to understand without trolling through thousands of rankings. NASTEA has the transparency to show what is going on under the hood: clear differences in narrative homogeneity.

## 8 Conclusion

We have shown that constraining document category can influence a model's performance on the cloze task. NASTEA, the new technique we have introduced to evaluate the properties of narrative schemas, paints a more complex picture: that some document categories—*Weddings* and *Obituaries*—are more homogeneous in the narratives they express than other sorts of categories. In other words, at the narratological level, not all categories are the same—some are measurably different from others. In the process, we have also defined the first ever measure for the presence of a schema in a document, opening up the possibility for techniques that use schemas to perform quantitative analysis of documents at the narratalogical level.

## Acknowledgments

We would like to thank Amir Zeldes, Nate Chambers, and the reviewers of this paper at multiple stages, whose feedback helped refine this work into its current form, as well as the Georgetown University Department of Linguistics and Graduate School for their continued support.

## References


Balasubramanian, N., Soderland, S., Mausam, & Etzioni, O. 2013. Generating Coherent Event Schemas at Scale. In *EMNLP* (pp. 1721-1731).

Bird, S., Loper, E., and Klein E. 2009. Natural Language Processing with Python. OReilly Media Inc.

Chambers, N., & Jurafsky, D. 2008. Unsupervised Learning of Narrative Event Chains. In *ACL* (pp. 789-797).

Chambers, N., & Jurafsky, D. 2009. Unsupervised learning of narrative schemas and their participants. *In Proceedings of the Joint Conference of the 47th Annual Meeting of the ACL and the 4th International Joint Conference on Natural Language Processing of the AFNLP: Volume 2-Volume 2* (pp. 602-610). Association for Computational Linguistics. Chicago

Chambers, N. W. 2011. Inducing Event Schemas and their Participants from Unlabeled Text. *Stanford University.*

Chambers, N. 2013. Event Schema Induction with a Probabilistic Entity-Driven Model. In *EMNLP* (pp. 1797-1807).

Cheung, J. C. K., Poon, H., & Vanderwende, L. 2013. Probabilistic frame induction. In *NAACL-HLT 2013* Association for Computational Linguistics.

de Marneffe, M., MacCartney, B., and Manning, C.D. 2006. Generating Typed Dependency Parses from Phrase Structure Parses. In *LREC 2006.*

Finkel, J.R., Grenager, T., and Manning, C. 2005. Incorporating Non-local Information into Information Extraction Systems by Gibbs Sampling. In *ACL 2005* (pp. 363-370).

Jans, B., Bethard, S., Vuli, I., & Moens, M. F. 2012. Skip n-grams and ranking functions for predicting script events. In *EACL* (pp. 336-344). Association for Computational Linguistics.

Lee, H., Chang, A., Peirsman, Y., Chambers, N., Surdeanu, M., and Jurafsky, D. 2013. Deterministic coreference resolution based on entity-centric, precision-ranked rules. *Computational Linguistics* 39(4).

Manning, C. D., Surdeanu, M., Bauer, J., Finkel, J., Bethard, S. J., and McClosky, D. 2014. The Stanford CoreNLP Natural Language Processing Toolkit. In *ACL* (System Demonstrations, pp. 55-60).

Miller, B., Olive, J., Gopavaram, S., & Shrestha, A. 2015. Cross-Document Non-Fiction Narrative Alignment. In *Proceedings of the First Workshop on Computing News Storylines* (pp. 56-61). Association for Computational Linguistics and The Asian Federation of Natural Language Processing.

Nguyen, K.H., Tannier, X., Ferret, O., & Besancon, R. 2015. Generative Event Schema Induction with Entity Disambiguation. In *ACL* (pp. 188 - 197)

Pichotta, K., & Mooney, R. J. 2014. Statistical Script Learning with Multi-Argument Events. In *EACL* (pp. 220-229).

Pichotta, K., & Mooney, R. J. 2015. Learning statistical scripts with LSTM recurrent neural networks. In *Proceedings of the 30th AAAI Conference on Artificial Intelligence.*

Sandhaus, E. 2008. *The New York Times Annotated Corpus.* Linguistic Data Consortium, Philadelphia.

Schank, R.C. & Abelson, R.P. 1977. Scripts, plans, goals and understanding. Lawrence Erlbaum.

Simonson, D. & Davis, A. 2015. Interactions between Narrative Schemas and Document Categories. In *Proceedings of the First Workshop on Computing News Storylines* (pp. 1-10). Association for Computational

Linguistics and The Asian Federation of Natural Language Processing.

Vossen, P., Caselli, T., & Kontzopoulou, Y. 2015. Storylines for structuring massive streams of news. In *Proceedings of the First Workshop on Computing News Storylines* (pp. 40-49). Association for Computational Linguistics and The Asian Federation of Natural Language Processing.

# The Storyline Annotation and Representation Scheme (StaR): A Proposal

**Tommaso Caselli** and **Piek Vossen**
Vrije Universiteit Amsterdam
De Boelelaan 1105 1081 HV Amsterdam (NL)
`{t.caselli;p.t.j.m.vossen}@vu.nl`

## Abstract

This paper illustrates a proposal for the development of an annotation scheme and a corpus for storyline extraction and evaluation from large collections of documents clustered around a topic. The scheme extends existing annotation efforts for event coreference and temporal processing, introducing additional layers and addressing shortcomings. We also show how a storyline can be derived from the annotated data.

## 1 Introduction

The stream of information is increasing every day posing difficult challenges for the selection and extraction of relevant information. Relevant information can be missed in this vast amount of data, leading to inconsistencies, fragmented reports, or gaps in the extraction and representation of complex stories. Different solutions have been proposed to deal with this problem ranging from the generation of multi-document extractive summaries (Barzilay et al., 1999), to clustering of news with respect to a topic (Swan and Allan, 2000), to the generation of timelines to monitor relevant events in a topic (Shahaf and Guestrin, 2010; Nguyen et al., 2014; Bauer and Teufel, 2015).

In this work, we want to expand on a different approach to select, organize, and represent relevant information from collections of documents clustered around a specific topic. Following Vossen et al. (2015), we adopt the storyline model as a representational device to structure the information, and aim at developing a reference corpus for a quantitative and qualitative evaluation of automatically generated storylines.

A storyline is as a structured index of chronologically ordered events which overcomes representation models based on pure timelines with respect to three aspects: i.) it is able to identify salient events (*climax events*) as the central elements around which a specific topic develops; ii.) it provides an explanatory model for how events connect to each other and contribute to the development of a topic; and iii.) it mimics a pervasive phenomenon in human life, i.e. the use of narrative strategies to organize and make sense of information.

Previous work in storyline generation is limited and in most cases what is labelled as a storyline is a timeline. The main difference is that storylines and narrative structures exhibit some causal and explanatory relation between events and some tension towards a resolution, or climax. We have identified four main contributions (Shahaf et al., 2013; Huang and Huang, 2013; Hu et al., 2014; Laparra et al., 2015) in this area proposing methods to generate storyline datasets. Although each contribution proposes its own definition of storyline, based on the sharing of participants, time and location, one of the commonalities of these works consists of the use of interactions and connections between cross-document topic threads or events which give rise to timelines, i.e. a basic temporal ordering.

Storylines also differ from Narrative Schemas (Chambers and Jurafsky, 2009). Narrative Schemas qualify as sets of partially ordered events with no distinction in relevance or salience



*Proceedings of 2nd Workshop on Computing News Storylines*, pages 67–72,
Austin, TX, November 5, 2016. ©2016 Association for Computational Linguistics

of their elements and, most importantly, with no explanatory power of the ways events are connected together, except for precedence relations. A Narrative Schema looks like an un-prioritized set of events which share some participants, thus leading to the development of entity-centric timelines. Furthermore, the use of entity driven relations (e.g. co-participation) to generate the schemas often result in non-coherent chains of events (Peng and Roth, 2016).

The remainder of this paper will be structured as follows: in Section 2 we will present the main aspects of the storyline model described in (Vossen et al., 2015) and show how these elements have been used to develop a proposal to annotate storylines. Section 3 will report on the preliminary application of the annotation scheme to a corpus presenting insights on the data and interaction between different layers of annotation ranging from event coreference to storyline. Finally, conclusions and future work will be reported in Section 4.

## 2 Annotating Storylines: A Proposal

The model described in Vossen et al. (2015) is grounded on the narratology framework of Bal (1997) which assumes that every narrative, regardless of the media and content, is a mention of a *fabula*, i.e., a sequence of chronologically ordered and logically connected events involving one or more actors. A *fabula* is a complex structure whose internal components can be decomposed in three main elements: i.) the *rising action(s)*, the event(s) that increases the tension created by a predicament; ii.) the *climax*, the event(s) which creates the maximal level of tension; and iii.) *falling action(s)*, the event(s) which resolve the climax and lower the narrative tension.

These narratological concepts have been translated in the storyline model by providing a definition and a formalization for the following basic components:

- events, participants (actors), locations and time-points (settings);
- the anchoring of events to time and their ordering (a timeline);
- bridging relations: a set of relations between events with explanatory and predictive value(s).

The proposed annotation scheme aims at grounding these concepts to linguistic elements in document collections. The scheme has been developed to maximize compatibility with existing annotation efforts on event and temporal processing, such as the Richer Event Description (RED) [1], THYME (Styler IV et al., 2014), and TimeML (Pustejovsky et al., 2003a), and event coreference, such as the Event CorefBank+ (ECB+) (Cybulska and Vossen, 2014b).

### 2.1 STaR: The Storyline Annotation and Representation Scheme

The Storyline Annotation and Representation Scheme (StaR) builds on and extends the ECB+ annotation scheme (Cybulska and Vossen, 2014a). The ECB+ scheme addresses event coreference both at the in- and cross-document levels. Event action coreference is specified as two action mentions which occur/hold true: i.) at the same time; ii.) in the same location; and iii.) with the same actors/participants. Thus, ECB+ data provides access to the first basic elements of the storyline model, i.e., events, participants (actors), locations, and time.

The timeline reconstruction is done by means of a temporal relation tag, `TLINK`, inheriting its semantics from TimeML. Although largely used and adapted to other languages, TimeML-annotated corpora suffer from sparse annotations and poorly connected event/time graphs. For instance, not every event mention is properly anchored to a temporal expression, nor are instructions on *when* annotated ordering relations between events clearly defined. In addition to this, the set of temporal relations adopted by TimeML is very fine-grained, with a total of 13 different values. To overcome these shortcomings of the TimeML annotation, we have designed our guidelines following two principles: i.) each event mention must be anchored to its time of occurrence; ii.) temporal ordering relations must be annotated only when in presence of linguistic evidence, thus limiting inferences. As such, no temporal relation should be annotated on the basis of world knowledge only.

---

[1] `https://goo.gl/iWUCFr`

Furthermore, the set of temporal values has been limited to 8 values (BEFORE, AFTER, OVERLAP, BEFORE_OVERLAP, BEGINS_ON, ENDS_ON, SIMULTANEOUS, INCLUDES). We also annotate temporal relations between events and the Document Creation Time (DCT). The DCT represents a special temporal anchor for actions which expresses a broad temporal dimension (e.g. Present, Past, or Future with respect the time the author created and published the text).

Following the proposal in Cassidy et al. (2014), we also annotate transitive closure relations between pairs of events to develop highly connected event graph. This means that in case of two pairs of events A BEFORE B and B BEFORE C, we explicitly mark the transitive closure relation A BEFORE C.

Finally, we extend the TLINK tag with the attribute contextualModality, from the RED scheme. It has 4 values: ACTUAL, UNCERTAIN, HYPOTHETICAL, and GENERIC. The attribute allows to represent claims of different sources concerning the reality or certainty of a temporal relation. The assignment of the contextual modality values is connected to the factuality profile of the events in the temporal relation but, at the same time, it is assumed to be independent from this latter aspect. The focus is on the factuality of the temporal relation itself. Consider the following examples from two documents about the 2013 Brooklyn riot from ECB+:

1. officers **shot** and killed a 16-year-old Kimani Gray in Brooklyn because he *allegedly* **pointed** a gun at the cops. [ecbplus19_10.xml - sentence 2]
   TLINK: pointed BEFORE shot - UNCERTAIN

2. Gray **pointed** a .38-caliber revolver at the cops before they **opened fire** [ecbplus19_4.xml - sentence 7]
   TLINK: pointed BEFORE opened fire - ACTUAL

ECB+ cross-document event coreference annotation tells us that both mentions of *pointed* are coreferential, as well as *shot* and *opened fire*. The time-line of the events is exactly the same, as expressed by the BEFORE relation, due to the presence of evidence such as "because" and "before". However,

the factuality of the TLINK is different in the two sources: in example 1. the temporal relation assumes an uncertain value while in example 2. is factual. Modeling these differences is a key element for storyline generation as these disagreements can be used to facilitate the identification of both relevant and interesting information and account for different perspectives on the same topic.

Bridging relations are modeled with a new link tag PLOT_LINK. The tag connects the event mentions in a document in order to reconstruct the tripartite structure of the *fabula*: rising actions, climax, and falling action. Two values are associated to the tag: PRECONDITION, which marks rising action relations, i.e., events which are circumstantial to, cause or enable another event, and FALLING_ACTION, which explicitly mark speculations and consequence relations, i.e. events which are the (anticipated) outcome or the effect of another event. The scheme is silent and neutral with respect to the climax event, i.e. no prior assumption is done. The identification of the climax event, or events, of the topic will emerge from the annotated data and it should correspond to the event(s) that has most incoming PRECONDITION (i.e. it is the target element of the relation) and/or outgoing FALLING_ACTION (i.e. it is the source element of the relation) links. PLOT_LINKs must be grounded on some evidence and not performed on the basis of world knowledge alone. In particular, two event mentions may stand in a PLOT_LINK relation if: i.) they share at least one participant (co-participation); or ii.) they stand in a causal or temporal relation; or iii.) if they stand in an entailment relation[2]. Recalling examples 1. and 2., the annotation of the PLOT_LINK is as follows:

1a source: *pointed* PRECONDITION target: *shot*
   source: *pointed* PRECONDITION target: *killed*
   source: *shot* FALLING_ACTION target: *killed*
2a source: *pointed* PRECONDITION target: *opened fire*

This will result in 3 PLOT_LINKs for the event *shot/opened fire* (2 PRECONDITION and 1

---

[2] We assume that not all co-participation relation may stand in an entailment relation.

FALLING_ACTION), 1 PLOT_LINKs for the event *killed*, and no PLOT_LINK for *pointed*. On the basis of the available data, *shot/opened fire* qualifies as the climax event.

## 3 The corpus: from ECB+ to ECBStaR

The ECB+ corpus contains 984 news articles and 43 topics, where each topic contains documents reporting on two different "seminal events" or topics. For instance, topic 19 in ECB+ contains two clusters of articles dealing with two different riots (one in Greece and one in Brooklyn). ECB+ annotation is performed through an event-centric approach. Only sentences containing mentions of the target seminal events were annotated, including any other event mention occurring in the same sentence. This has lead to a relevance based annotation: only a subset of the sentences in a document is annotated, i.e., those mentioning the target topic, while the rest is ignored. All event mentions in the selected sentences are annotated, not only those explicitly referring to the target topic. The outcome of this approach resulted in 3,487 annotated event mentions, with 2,050 coreference relations (in- and cross-document).

In Figure 1 we graphically illustrate how storylines can be reconstructed as an outcome of the annotation and interaction between the different layers. The top part of the figure contains sentences from different articles. To simplify the representation, we have only marked events (in bold) and temporal expressions (in italics). The bottom part of the picture contains a representation for event coferece, timeline, and storyline. by creating unique representations (i.e. instance identifiers).

Each document timeline is merged together into a unique topic/seminal event timeline based on the event coreference data. Timeline representation follows the event-centric annotation of ECB+ but enriches it with time anchoring and ordering relations. In particular: i.) each event instance is associated to its correct time anchor (e.g. "2013-03-09 E1"); ii.) ordering relations based on precedence relations (i.e., BEFORE or AFTER) among instances are represented with numerical indexes (e.g. "1 2013-03-09 E1" -"2 2013-03-09 E6"). In case other types of temporal relations hold between pairs of events, the same numerical index is assigned to

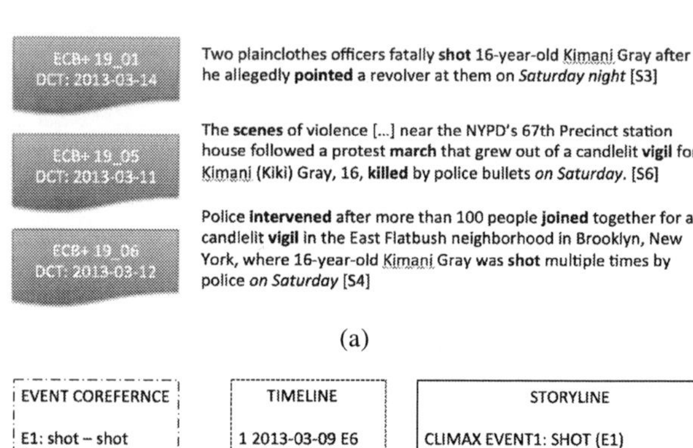


(a)

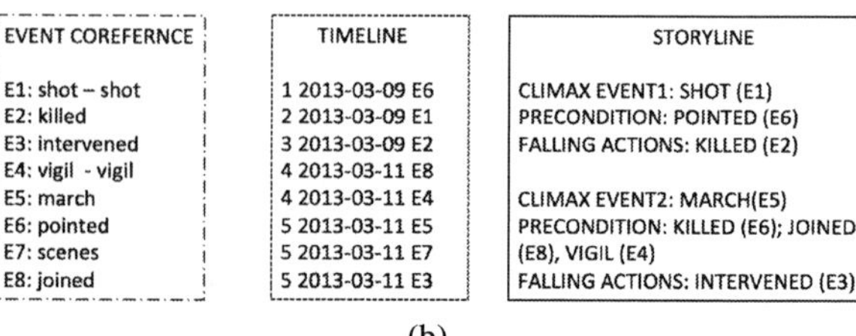

| EVENT COREFERNCE | TIMELINE | STORYLINE |
|---|---|---|
| E1: shot – shot | 1 2013-03-09 E6 | CLIMAX EVENT1: SHOT (E1) |
| E2: killed | 2 2013-03-09 E1 | PRECONDITION: POINTED (E6) |
| E3: intervened | 3 2013-03-09 E2 | FALLING ACTIONS: KILLED (E2) |
| E4: vigil - vigil | 4 2013-03-11 E8 | |
| E5: march | 4 2013-03-11 E4 | CLIMAX EVENT2: MARCH(E5) |
| E6: pointed | 5 2013-03-11 E5 | PRECONDITION: KILLED (E6); JOINED |
| E7: scenes | 5 2013-03-11 E7 | (E8), VIGIL (E4) |
| E8: joined | 5 2013-03-11 E3 | FALLING ACTIONS: INTERVENED (E3) |

(b)

Figure 1: Storyline reconstruction and representation.

all events. The specific temporal value is not lost and can be accessed by inspecting the binary relations between the events [3]. Finally, on the basis of the PLOT_LINK annotations, a storyline can be reconstructed. In our specific case, we have identified 2 climax events ("shot" and "march") as both events obtained the same score. Each climax event is then associated to a list PRECONDITIONs and/or FALLING_ACTIONS. The connection between climax events is guaranteed by the timeline data. Furthermore, it is interesting to notice that climax identification is not based on the number of event mentions (i.e., the event with highest number of mentions in the document collection) but on the information derived from PLOT_LINKs.

The annotation effort to develop the ECBStaR corpus is still at an early stage. So far, only 3 seminal events[4] for which the DCT was available have been enriched with TLINKs and PLOT_LINKs, resulting in 33 annotated documents, 3 storylines (one per seminal events), 1,229 TLINKs, 317 PLOT_LINKs, with 223 falling action relations, 46 precondition relations, and 5 climax events. The first interesting data concerns the amount of TLINKs. Storyline annotation aims at creating densely connected temporal relation graphs, to avoid shortcomings of

---

[3]This is not illustrated in the figure to facilitate the reading.

[4]The seminal events corresponds to the ECB+ data for topics 19, 37, and 41.

previous temporal annotation initiatives based on TimeML which lacked densed connections among the annotated data.

Concerning the `PLOT_LINK` annotation, the large amount of falling action relations can be explained by taking into account two factors. The first concerns the nature of news data. News is published quickly, and often information about preconditions are lacking or irrelevant. Furthermore, in case of long lasting stories, such as wars, we have access to a limited set of articles concerning a specif sub-event (in our case the bombing in a South Sudan refugee camp - topic 41), thus preventing the identification of rising action relations because this information is considered to be active in the shared knowledge and irrelevant for the current document. The second factor concerns the specific topic which gives rise to the storyline. For instance, natural disaster storylines will barely have mentions of precondition actions as most of the time natural disasters are reported as things that simply occur.

## 4    Conclusion and Future Work

This paper reports on a proposal of an annotation scheme to develop a reference corpus for storylines from large document collections. The availability of a such a reference corpus will allow a qualitative and quantitative evaluation of storylines, taking into account the two key dimensions: timelines and *fabula*, i.e., the identification of the climax events and the explanatory connections with other events.

One additional insight we hope to achieve with the ECBStaR corpus is the identification of specialized event patterns for different storylines, thus contributing to new models of knowledge template acquisition.

Finally, we are planning to extend the collected data per topic in time. In particular, we aim at harvesting additional documents related to each seminal events to extend the time span of the topic and better monitor the evolution of the story.

## References


Mieke Bal. 1997. *Narratology: Introduction to the theory of narrative.* University of Toronto Press.

Regina Barzilay, Kathleen R McKeown, and Michael Elhadad. 1999. Information fusion in the context of multi-document summarization. In *Proceedings of the 37th annual meeting of the Association for Computational Linguistics on Computational Linguistics*, pages 550–557. Association for Computational Linguistics.

Sandro Bauer and Simone Teufel. 2015. A methodology for evaluating timeline generation algorithms based on deep semantic units. In *Proceedings of the 53rd Annual Meeting of the Association for Computational Linguistics and the 7th International Joint Conference on Natural Language Processing (Volume 2: Short Papers)*, pages 834–839, Beijing, China, July. Association for Computational Linguistics.

Taylor Cassidy, Bill McDowell, Nathanael Chambers, and Steven Bethard. 2014. An annotation framework for dense event ordering. In *Proceedings of the 52nd Annual Meeting of the Association for Computational Linguistics (Volume 2: Short Papers)*, pages 501–506, Baltimore, Maryland, June. Association for Computational Linguistics.

Nathanael Chambers and Dan Jurafsky. 2009. Unsupervised learning of narrative schemas and their participants. In *Proceedings of the Joint Conference of the 47th Annual Meeting of the ACL and the 4th International Joint Conference on Natural Language Processing of the AFNLP: Volume 2 Volume 2*, pages 602–610. Association for Computational Linguistics.

Agata Cybulska and Piek Vossen. 2014a. Guidelines for ECB+ annotation of events and their coreference. Technical Report NWR-2014-1, VU University Amsterdam.

Agata Cybulska and Piek Vossen. 2014b. Using a sledgehammer to crack a nut? Lexical diversity and event coreference resolution. In *Proceedings of the 9th Language Resources and Evaluation Conference (LREC2014)*, Reykjavik, Iceland, May 26-31.

Po Hu, Min-Lie Huang, and Xiao-Yan Zhu. 2014. Exploring the interactions of storylines from informative news events. *Journal of Computer Science and Technology*, 29(3):502–518.

Lifu Huang and Lian'en Huang. 2013. Optimized event storyline generation based on mixture-event-aspect model. In *Proceedings of the 2013 Conference on Empirical Methods in Natural Language Processing*, pages 726–735, Seattle, Washington, USA, October. Association for Computational Linguistics.

Egoitz Laparra, Itziar Aldabe, and German Rigau. 2015. From timelines to storylines: A preliminary proposal for evaluating narratives. In *Proceedings of the First Workshop on Computing News Storylines*, pages 50–55, Beijing, China, July. Association for Computational Linguistics.

Kiem-Hieu Nguyen, Xavier Tannier, and Veronique Moriceau. 2014. Ranking multidocument event descriptions for building thematic timelines. In *Proceedings of COLING '14*, pages 1208–1217.

Haoruo Peng and Dan Roth. 2016. Two discourse driven language models for semantics. In *Proceedings of the 54th Annual Meeting of the Association for Computational Linguistics (Volume 1: Long Papers)*, pages 290–300, Berlin, Germany, August. Association for Computational Linguistics.

James Pustejovsky, José Castao, Robert Ingria, Roser Saurì, Robert Gaizauskas, Andrea Setzer, and Graham Katz. 2003a. TimeML: Robust Specification of Event and Temporal Expressions in Text. In *Fifth International Workshop on Computational Semantics (IWCS-5)*.

Dafna Shahaf and Carlos Guestrin. 2010. Connecting the dots between news articles. In *Proceedings of the 16th ACM SIGKDD international conference on Knowledge discovery and data mining*, pages 623–632. ACM.

Dafna Shahaf, Jaewon Yang, Caroline Suen, Jeff Jacobs, Heidi Wang, and Jure Leskovec. 2013. Information cartography: creating zoomable, large-scale maps of information. In *Proceedings of the 19th ACM SIGKDD international conference on Knowledge discovery and data mining*, pages 1097–1105. ACM.

William F Styler IV, Steven Bethard, Sean Finan, Martha Palmer, Sameer Pradhan, Piet C de Groen, Brad Erickson, Timothy Miller, Chen Lin, Guergana Savova, et al. 2014. Temporal annotation in the clinical domain. *Transactions of the Association for Computational Linguistics*, 2:143–154.

Russell Swan and James Allan. 2000. Automatic generation of overview timelines. In *Proceedings of the 23rd annual international ACM SIGIR conference on Research and development in information retrieval*, pages 49–56. ACM.

Piek Vossen, Tommaso Caselli, and Yiota Kontzopoulou. 2015. Storylines for structuring massive streams of news. In *Proceedings of the First Workshop on Computing News Storylines*, pages 40–49, Beijing, China, July. Association for Computational Linguistics.

# Author Index

**Association for Computational Linguistics**
209 N. Eighth Street
Stroudsburg, Pennsylvania 18360

ISBN 978-1-5108-3149-0